WEEKDAY PRAYERS

Donal Harrington

Weekday Prayers

Prayers for Weekday Masses and Prayer Services

the columba press

First published in 2013 by
the columba press
55A Spruce Avenue,
Stillorgan Industrial Park,
Blackrock, Co. Dublin

Cover by Bill Bolger
Origination by The Columba Press
Printed by Sprint-Print Ltd

ISBN 978 1 78218 117 0

All rights reserved. Without limiting the rights under copyright reserved alone, no part of this publication may be reproduced, stored in or introduced into a retrieval system, or transmitted, in any form or by any means (electronic, mechanical, photocopying, recording or otherwise) without the prior written permission of both the copyright owner and the above publisher of this book.

The Scripture quotations contained herein are from the New Revised Standard Version Bible, copyright © 1989, Division of Christian Education of the National Council of Churches of Christ in the U.S.A. Used by permission. All rights reserved.

Copyright © 2013, Donal Harrington

Table of Contents

Introduction	7
Advent	9
Christmas	23
Lent	33
Easter	55
Ordinary Time	79
Feasts	183
Scripture Index	213

Introduction

These prayers are intended to enhance the quality of prayer at weekday Masses and prayer services. For each day there is an introduction plus two prayers of the faithful. These are based on the gospel of the day. The introduction uses a theme from the gospel to invite those gathered into a quiet prayer moment at the start of Mass. The two prayers of the faithful draw further meanings from the gospel in the form of intercessions for those present and/or the wider community.

So the heart of it is the gospel. Not a book of random intercessions, but a sustained attempt to enter into contemplation of the day's gospel passage. In a sense, the two prayers of the faithful for each day are a kind of 'homily' in the form of prayer. What I mean is that they are the outcome of meditating on the meanings that arise from the text. They cast that meditation in the form of prayer. In that way the prayers seek to make connections between the gospel and daily life.

The relevance of this is wider than daily Mass. With less priests there are now less Masses. On more and more weekdays, there will be a prayer service instead of Mass, led by members of the congregation themselves. This book offers itself as a resource in that context, helping parishes to make such prayer services into an enriching exploration of the day's gospel. Thereby, perhaps, the worshipping community may grow in its familiarity with and understanding of the gospels.

The texts included here are not set in stone. Hopefully people will feel free to adapt them to suit themselves. The person leading the prayer will want to be comfortable with the text, and that may call for rewording or editing. The main thing is not to use the text unthinkingly. Rather, it is meant as a help for the leader of the liturgy in their own contemplation of the gospel.

Introductions and prayers are provided for all the weekdays of Ordinary Time, Advent and Christmas, Lent and Easter. There are also introductions and prayers for solemnities and feasts, as well as for selected saints' days through the year.

For most of the year, only the gospel is used as a source of prayer. This is because Ordinary Time has a one-year cycle of gospels, but a two-year cycle of first readings.

My book *Eucharist: Enhancing the Prayer* (Columba, 2007) is a companion volume. It contains sets of prayers of the faithful for Sundays and for various occasions during the year. Its index of Scripture references means that it can also be drawn upon as an additional resource for weekdays.

As with that book, *Weekday Prayers* owes much to the ideas and encouragement of John O'Connell and Donal O'Doherty. Thanks to you both!

Advent

WEEK ONE – MONDAY

Matthew 8:5–11 (the centurion)

Introduction to Mass
We begin with the words of the centurion in today's gospel – words that we say at Communion – 'Lord, I am not worthy'. May those words encourage us now to allow God come near and touch us in our need.

Prayers of the Faithful
Jesus says, 'Nowhere have I found faith like this'. As Advent begins, we pray for new faith in what God can do in our lives. We pause to think of what we want Jesus to do for us.

Jesus invites each of us to his table. He makes each of us a guest worthy to be here. May all who feel unworthy be able to say 'Yes' to his invitation.

WEEK ONE – TUESDAY

Luke 10:21–24 ('happy the eyes')

Introduction to Mass
We begin with Jesus' words in our gospel, 'Happy the eyes that see what you see'. Happy are we, called to his supper. Let us be silent for a moment in God's presence, and become aware of our happiness in the Lord.

Prayers of the Faithful
We thank God for what we see – for what the eyes of faith show us: the love of God revealed to us in Jesus Christ. May we live in a spirit of gratitude.

We pray for peace among the nations of the earth. May Christ's spirit enter into people's hearts this Advent, and dispel thoughts of conquest, hatred and revenge.

WEEK ONE – WEDNESDAY

Matthew 15:29–37 ('I feel sorry for all these people')

Introduction to Mass
We bring our needs and our tears to the Lord, who says in the gospel, 'I feel sorry for all these people'. We pray quietly that the Lord will reach out and touch us.

Prayers of the Faithful
In Jesus, we are in touch with God's dream for humanity – a world where suffering is healed and where everybody has enough. May Jesus' Spirit, within us and among us, make us passionate to bring this about.

We thank God for the people through whom Christ comes to us each day – family and neighbours, friends and strangers.

WEEK ONE – THURSDAY

Matthew 7:21, 24–27 (house built on rock)

Introduction to Mass
A quiet moment to begin. The gospel is the story of the house built on rock. With our worries and troubles, we pause to become aware of God, our rock, our foundation, our security.

Prayers of the Faithful
We pray this Advent for a faith that is alive and active, that shows itself in the choices we make and in the way we treat others.

Thinking of the image of the floods and gales, we pray for people who have lost their homes. We pray for victims of landslides or earthquakes, flooding or storms.

WEEK ONE – FRIDAY

Matthew 9:27–31 (two blind men)

Introduction to Mass
In the gospel two blind men ask Jesus to help them. We start Mass with a simple question: What do I want Jesus to do for me? We stay quietly with that question for a moment.

Prayers of the Faithful
The blind men lead us to think of all whose vision is impaired and all whose sight is getting weaker. We hope God's Spirit and the encouragement of others will help them to cope.

May the Lord's coming be a time of grace. May people become more confident and less fearful – more free and less anxious.

WEEK ONE – SATURDAY

Matthew 9:35–10:1, 6–8 (Jesus calls the twelve)

Introduction to Mass
In the gospel Jesus calls the twelve apostles. He calls each of us too. We begin our Mass by being quiet so that we can hear his call in our hearts.

Prayers of the Faithful
Jesus calls the twelve – and he calls each one of us too – to get involved in his work. This Advent, may we listen anew and hear his call with new ears.

Jesus cured all kinds of sickness and diseases. We pray that his compassion will grow in our hearts, to make us more sensitive and responsive to others.

WEEK TWO – MONDAY

Luke 5:17–26 (a paralysed man)

Introduction to Mass
We begin our Mass with a quiet moment. In the gospel a man is carried to Jesus. We think of the people who have carried us in our need, and we give thanks to God for them.

Prayers of the Faithful
Of all Jesus' healings and wonders, the greatest wonder is forgiveness – the good news that we are forgiven by God, accepted and cherished as we are. May we believe this and take heart from it this Advent.

Thinking of the paralysed man, we pray for all among us with reduced mobility and for all who are housebound. We thank God that they can still be a blessing to others around them.

WEEK TWO – TUESDAY

Matthew 18:12–14 (the lost sheep)

Introduction to Mass
Thinking of the lost sheep in today's gospel, we start our celebration by thinking of somebody we know who is lost or out in the cold. We bring them into our prayer.

Prayers of the Faithful
We praise God for such inclusive love, embracing all, excluding nobody. We ask this Advent for a share of God's Spirit, to inspire our own attitudes to others.

Sometimes we despair that someone we know has been lost to God. May we be encouraged by Jesus' words, and let despair give way to hope.

WEEK TWO – WEDNESDAY

Matthew 11:28–30 ('come to me')

Introduction to Mass
In the gospel Jesus says, 'Come to me'. For a quiet moment we come near to him, with whatever is worrying us or weighing us down.

Prayers of the Faithful
We pray for all who labour and are overburdened, all who are bowed down with burdens and expectations, all who are made to carry a heavy load. May Jesus comfort them.

Jesus promises rest for our souls. This Advent we ask him to help us to take time to stop, to stand back, to reflect and to pray.

WEEK TWO – THURSDAY

Matthew 11:11–15 (John the Baptist)

Introduction to Mass
With today's gospel, our thoughts turn to John the Baptist, who prepares the people for the advent of Christ. We open our hearts to his invitation. Come to us, Lord, this Advent. Make your home within us and among us.

Prayers of the Faithful
We think for a moment of whatever it is that we are waiting for this Advent – whatever it is that we are yearning for. We offer our waiting and yearning to the Lord.

For a good many people, Christmas is not a happy time – bereavement, loneliness, troubles. We reach out to them with our prayer and our care.

WEEK TWO – FRIDAY

Matthew 11:16–19 ('the Son of Man comes eating and drinking')

Introduction to Mass
Jesus is our hope and our joy, as today's gospel suggests to us. In a moment of quiet now, let us allow his hope and joy penetrate into our hearts.

Prayers of the Faithful
This is how some people saw Jesus – 'eating and drinking, a glutton and a drunkard, a friend of tax-collectors and sinners'. It suggests the mood about him was one of joy and celebration. May we have that same mood. May Jesus' coming bring us joy and give us cause for celebration.

The gospel suggests how small-minded and ungracious Jesus found some people to be. May our own response to him be open, appreciative and generous.

WEEK TWO – SATURDAY

Matthew 17:10–13 (Elijah and John the Baptist)

Introduction to Mass
There is a saying about prayer: 'Better a heart without words than words without heart'. So let us be silent for a moment, our hearts empty for the Lord.

Prayers of the Faithful
By connecting John the Baptist with Elijah, the gospel points to Jesus, our promised Messiah. This Advent, may our hearts turn to him and grow in expectation.

Advent is about waiting. We think of people who are waiting – waiting for news, waiting for somebody, waiting for something to change. By the grace of Advent, may all who are waiting be able to wait in hope.

WEEK THREE – MONDAY

Matthew 21:23–27 ('what authority have you?')

Introduction to Mass
Jesus, in our gospel, shows himself as the presence and power of God. Let us rest a moment with him, to feel that presence and power.

Prayers of the Faithful
Today's gospel is about the authority of Jesus, about recognising that he truly comes from God. May God enlighten the eyes of our mind, to see ever more clearly who Jesus really is.

As we continue on our Advent journey, we ask God to purify the faith of all who are wavering or struggling. May their faith become more sincere and assured.

WEEK THREE – TUESDAY

Matthew 21:28–32 (the two sons)

Introduction to Mass
We have a story in today's gospel about having the courage to change and repent. I invite you to share quietly with Jesus one way in which you would like to change for the better.

Prayers of the Faithful
Thinking of these two sons, may we be able to change our mind and admit when we are wrong. May the Lord keep us from pride and self-righteousness.

Jesus says, 'I tell you solemnly, tax-collectors and prostitutes are making their way into the kingdom of God before you'. Lord, gives us eyes to see your grace even in the most unlikely people. Teach us to be humble.

WEEK THREE – WEDNESDAY

Luke 7:19–23 ('tell John what you have seen')

Introduction to Mass
We gather to give thanks. So let us begin with a quiet pause to think; what do I want to give thanks for? Let us share that with the Lord.

Prayers of the Faithful
With John the Baptist, we ask of Jesus: 'Are you the one who is to come or have we to wait for someone else?' May this Advent give us deeper faith in Jesus, a stronger assurance that he is the one sent by God.

May all Christians share Jesus' spirit of preferential care for people who are disadvantaged, deprived, disabled or despised. May others hear the good news in and through our care.

WEEK THREE – THURSDAY

Luke 7:24–30 ('no one greater than John')

Introduction to Mass
John the Baptist features again in our gospel today. In the spirit of his message, let us silently open our hearts and prepare the way for the Lord to enter in.

Prayers of the Faithful
We thank God for John the Baptist, the prophet who leads people to Jesus. We thank God for the people in our own lives who lead us to Jesus and who show us the way.

Jesus says that some people 'thwarted what God had in mind for them'. We ask: what does God have in mind for me? Let us open our hearts this Advent and find out with joy what God has in mind for us.

WEEK THREE – FRIDAY

John 5:33–36 ('John was a lamp')

Introduction to Mass
Jesus tells us that the Father has sent him. Let us pray quietly for open hearts, to receive God's gift to us this Christmas.

Prayers of the Faithful
'John was a lamp, alight and shining'. May John the Baptist shine light on our path this Advent. May he point us to Jesus. May we be drawn closer to Jesus.

We thank God for people in our world who are a lamp, alight and shining. We thank God for people who let their light shine, who bring light and hope to others.

17 DECEMBER

Matthew 1:1–17 (genealogy of Jesus)

Introduction to Mass
As we listen to today's gospel list the generations down to the birth of Jesus, we can feel his coming closer. We become quiet for a moment. We become aware of the life of Jesus that is growing within each of us.

Prayers of the Faithful
There's a sense in today's gospel of everything leading to Christ. May everything in our lives lead to him too. May he be the centre of our lives.

We hear so many great names – Abraham and Jacob, David and Solomon. And many more unfamiliar to us. As we listen, we pray for the Jewish people, with whom we share so much in our faith and our religion.

18 DECEMBER

Matthew 1:18–24 (Joseph)

Introduction to Mass
Today in the gospel we hear the word 'Emmanuel', God-with-us. Let us rest for a moment with that word as we begin … Emmanuel, God with us.

Prayers of the Faithful
Today's gospel brings Joseph before us – his honour and integrity; his courage to let God's Spirit guide him into something unknown. May something of the spirit of Joseph fall on us today, to soothe our fear and give us courage.

'They will call him Emmanuel, God-with-us.' May the words sink deep into our hearts – God is with me. We think of the Irish greeting, 'Dia dhuit'; God be with you. We make that our prayer for all whom we meet today.

19 DECEMBER

Luke 1:5–25 (Zechariah and Elizabeth)

Introduction to Mass
In yesterday's gospel an angel came to Joseph. In today's, an angel comes to Zechariah. In tomorrow's, the angel will visit Mary. To each of them the angel says, 'Do not be afraid'. Let us feel God reaching out to us too, as Christmas approaches, saying to each of us, 'Do not be afraid'.

Prayers of the Faithful
Thinking of Zechariah and Elizabeth in today's gospel, we pause for a moment. We look over the years of our own lives, how God has been with us and carried us through all the ups and downs. We say 'thanks'.

As we hear about Elizabeth, we think of women who are childless and of couples who want a child of their own. May they hear good news in their lives.

20 DECEMBER

Luke 1:26–38 (the angel Gabriel visits Mary)

Introduction to Mass
The angel's words to Mary in today's gospel are also God's words to us – 'Rejoice, so highly favoured'. Let us take these words into the quiet of our hearts – 'Rejoice, so highly favoured'.

Prayers of the Faithful
Mary said 'Yes' to the angel. May we too say 'Yes'; may Christ be born in us this Christmas.

We pray for people who are afraid – afraid of something happening, or something going wrong, or afraid to be themselves, or whatever. May God send angels to comfort all who are afraid.

21 DECEMBER

Luke 1:39–45 (Mary visits Elizabeth)

Introduction to Mass
The story today of the Visitation is a story of hospitality. It reminds us of the spirit of hospitality in the Mass. God welcomes us here as cherished guests. And we open our hearts to welcome God in a moment of quiet.

Prayers of the Faithful
May Mary visiting Elizabeth encourage us to visit, to renew our contact with somebody, to rediscover someone we are out of touch with.

With Mary and Elizabeth, we pray for all mothers and for all who are carrying a child this Christmas. We rejoice at how their special experience gives them a unique insight into Christmas.

22 DECEMBER

Luke 1:46–56 (Mary's Magnificat)

Introduction to Mass
In the spirit of Mary's Magnificat, we begin Mass by reaching out in quiet prayer to touch those who are hungry, poor or downtrodden. We embrace them quietly with our prayer.

Prayers of the Faithful
May God, who exalted Mary in her lowliness, be the hope of all who are bowed down, and the strength of all who are humble.

We rejoice with Mary in the great things God has done for her. We rejoice in what God has done for us through her. With Mary we proclaim the greatness of the Lord.

23 DECEMBER

Luke 1:57–66 (birth of John the Baptist)

Introduction to Mass
Today's gospel begins with Zechariah still silent. We begin our prayer in silence, with him, opening our deepest selves to the Lord.

Prayers of the Faithful
May the birth of John the Baptist help us this Christmas to appreciate the wonder of our being and the wonder of our calling.

We pray for our children. May they be blessed with the joy of Christmas. May we all go out of our way to share joy.

24 DECEMBER

Luke 1:67–79 (Benedictus)

Introduction to Mass
Zechariah's Benedictus prayer ends with the words, 'guide our feet into the way of peace'. For a quiet moment, we become aware of God's peace within us, deeper than our own hearts.

Prayers of the Faithful
We feel the assurance in Zechariah's prayer, assurance that the Lord has visited his people. May that assurance come to all of us in a new way this Christmas.

In the words of Zechariah we pray; may the rising Sun come to visit us, to give light to all who live in darkness and in the shadow of death.

Christmas

26 DECEMBER

St Stephen

Introduction to Mass
Our gospel on this feast of St Stephen tells us never to worry about what to say, that God's Spirit will give us words and will speak through us. We open our hearts now to receive this inspiration of God.

Prayers of the Faithful
St Stephen was the first Christian martyr. May our first inclination as Christians be to give of ourselves and to share the joy we so gratefully receive at Christmas.

St Stephen is the patron saint of deacons. We pray for all who serve as deacons in our parishes. May their Christian witness inspire in us all a spirit of service.

27 DECEMBER

St John

Introduction to Mass
On this feast of St John, the gospel describes him as the disciple whom Jesus loved. In the quiet of our hearts let us hear those words being said of ourselves – I am the disciple whom Jesus loves.

Prayers of the Faithful
We thank God for John, author of the fourth gospel, perhaps best known for giving us Jesus' commandment to love one another – this simple, powerful expression of the essence of Christianity.

The gospel presents John as one of the first to experience Jesus' resurrection. We ask God to give us a share of his enthusiasm, his joy, his amazement.

28 DECEMBER

Holy Innocents

Introduction to Mass
In today's gospel, on the feast of the holy innocents, Joseph is again guided by an angel. In the peace of our hearts, let us listen to God's angel, guiding us which way to go.

Prayers of the Faithful
The joy of Christ being born is quickly followed by the horror of innocent children being slaughtered. That is the world we live in – the light and the darkness. May we all be active co-workers in Christ's light overcoming the darkness.

We pray for children who are suffering from torture, cruelty, violence. We pray for those who are weakest and most vulnerable amongst us.

29 DECEMBER

Luke 2:22–35 (Simeon)

Introduction to Mass
In the gospel today, Jesus' parents bring him to present him to the Lord. We begin our prayer by presenting ourselves. We quietly ask God to receive the gift of ourselves.

Prayers of the Faithful
Simeon rejoices to have finally seen God's salvation. We pray for all who are waiting for God. We pray that many will, like Simeon, find the fulfilment of their hopes in Christ.

Simeon says to Mary, 'a sword will pierce your own soul too'. We think of mothers among us who are anxious over their children. May they find strength and comfort in Mary.

30 DECEMBER

Luke 2:36–40 (Anna)

Introduction to Mass
Today's gospel praises God for the coming of Christ. We begin our Eucharist – our thanksgiving – with a quiet moment thanking God for Christ, who has come into our lives and our world.

Prayers of the Faithful
84 year old Anna praises God. We thank God for older people among us who, like Anna, have grown to appreciate so much God's coming among us in Christ.

May the words spoken of the young Jesus be true of all our growing children – may God's favour be with them and may they be filled with wisdom.

31 DECEMBER

John 1:1–18 (the Word)

Introduction to Mass
In the gospel today we hear, 'the Word became flesh and lived among us'. We rest quietly with these words for a moment – God has come near to us, God has made God's home with us and within us.

Prayers of the Faithful
As the year ends, we give thanks for God's blessings – in the words of the gospel, 'from his fulness we have all of us received, grace in return for grace'.

The light shines in the darkness, a light the darkness could not overcome. We pray for all who are going through dark times. We pray for the light of Christ in the year ahead, to enlighten us and to conquer our darkness.

1 JANUARY

Mary Mother of God

Introduction to Mass
Celebrating this feast, we recall why God's Son was born of a woman – it was so that we might all be born into God. We pause with this thought: Mary gave birth to the Son of God, and we are born into God.

Prayers of the Faithful
Thinking of Mary today, we pray for mothers, and we praise God. For they, like Mary, bring life and hope into the world. May we all be like Mary; may we all be a life-giving, hope-filled presence wherever we go.

Looking to the year ahead, may each of us have peace in our hearts. May each of us increase the peace in the world. We think quietly of people we know, and we wish them peace in the coming year.

2 JANUARY

John 1:19–28 (John the Baptist)

Introduction to Mass
In the gospel we hear the words of Isaiah, 'make a straight way for the Lord'. We open our hearts as we begin our prayer. We make a path to our hearts for the Lord to enter in.

Prayers of the Faithful
'There stands among you, unknown to you, the one who is coming.' We pray that we will be aware and attentive and vigilant, to recognise Christ who comes among us in so many different ways.

The next few days' gospels are about Jesus meeting his first disciples. We pray, as this new year begins, that we will meet him anew. May our relationship to Jesus be refreshed and renewed.

3 JANUARY

John 1:29–34 (lamb of God)

Introduction to Mass
In the gospel, John the Baptist says, 'there is the lamb of God who takes away the sin of the world'. We come before the lamb in our weakness. We pray for his forgiving Spirit to fill us and take away our sin.

Prayers of the Faithful
We pray for Christ's Spirit to rest on all Christians and to strengthen them. May all Christians play their part in opposing the power of sin in the world.

John proclaims that Jesus is the chosen one of God. May the year ahead be a journey of discovery for us, discovering in new ways who Jesus is.

4 JANUARY

John 1:35–42 ('come and see')

Introduction to Mass
Today's gospel tells us about Jesus' first disciples. In the silence of our hearts, let us hear once more Jesus' calling each of us to be his disciples.

Prayers of the Faithful
Jesus asks, 'what do you want?' May Jesus lead us to discover the deepest needs and desires within ourselves. May Jesus increase our desire for God.

Jesus says, 'come and see'. May we respond to his invitation and spend time with him in prayer and meditation, getting to know him better.

5 JANUARY

John 1:43–51 (Philip, Nathanael)

Introduction to Mass
In our gospel, Nathanael is surprised that Jesus already knows him before they meet. Jesus knows us too, better than we know ourselves. We pause for a moment in the security of that thought.

Prayers of the Faithful
Philip meets Jesus and then introduces Nathanael to him. We too are blessed to have met Jesus. We pray for courage to introduce Jesus to others, in whatever way we can.

Philip says, 'we have found the One about whom the prophets wrote'. May we have a share of his excitement. May we find Jesus each day as if for the first time.

6 JANUARY

The Epiphany

Introduction to Mass
On this feast, Christ is revealed as the light of the world. Let us now come into God's presence, and allow ourselves to be bathed in that light.

Prayers of the Faithful
We pray for each person here. As each of us follows our star, may we find Christ in our lives this coming year. As with the wise men, may the light of Christ fill us with delight.

As the Christmas season culminates today, we give thanks for the new sense of God's closeness given to us this Christmas. May the world recognise the light of Christ, and may all people be united in God.

7 JANUARY

Matthew 4:12–17, 23–25 (Jesus begins his preaching)

Introduction to Mass
We hear Jesus' first words in the gospel today: 'Repent, the kingdom is at hand'. Let us be quiet – God is near – drawing us towards him. Let us let go of sin and turn to him.

Prayers of the Faithful
We see Jesus leaving home and beginning his ministry. We pray for people who are leaving home to start out on their own path. May God's Spirit go with them. May Jesus be their inspiration.

We pray for all among us who, like those in today's gospel, are sick or suffering. We pray for Jesus' healing and strengthening. May we ourselves grow in awareness and compassion.

8 JANUARY

Mark 6:34–44 (loaves and fishes)

Introduction to Mass
Our gospel sees Jesus take pity on the people; they are like sheep without a shepherd. Let us imagine that we are those people. We know how we can be lost or needy. For a silent moment we feel Jesus taking pity on us.

Prayers of the Faithful
Part of the miracle of the loaves and fishes is that so little could be enough. When we feel that we have little to offer, when we feel helpless or inadequate, may what we have be transformed by Jesus, and become enough.

We think of the hunger of so many in our world. May we, who are blessed with this food from heaven, do all we can to increase the sharing and generosity in the world.

9 JANUARY

Mark 6:45–52 (walking on water)

Introduction to Mass
In our gospel, when Jesus gets into the boat with the disciples, the wind drops and there is calm. We now quietly allow Jesus come into our hearts, to bring calm amidst our troubles.

Prayers of the Faithful
May each of us, whatever our concerns at the moment, take heart from Jesus' words, 'Courage. It is I. Do not be afraid'.

We think of someone we know who is afraid or struggling. We pray that we can bring something of Jesus' calming presence to them.

10 JANUARY

Luke 4:14–22 ('the Spirit of the Lord has been given to me')

Introduction to Mass
The gospel today says that all eyes in the synagogue were fixed on Jesus. Let it be the same here. In silence let us fix our eyes on Jesus, who looks lovingly on us.

Prayers of the Faithful
May we offer ourselves to share generously in Jesus' mission, his reaching out to the poor and the captive, the disabled and the downtrodden. Lord, give us a share of your Spirit.

The gospel talks about 'the gracious words that came from his lips'. May the words we speak be gracious – words of comfort, words of hope, words of kindness and encouragement.

11 JANUARY

Luke 5:12–16 (a leper)

Introduction to Mass
The man with leprosy in today's gospel approaches Jesus, wanting to be healed. We approach Jesus too, in the silence of our hearts. We bring him our need, our wanting to be healed.

Prayers of the Faithful
Thinking of the man's leprosy, we pray for all who suffer from diseases of the skin, for all whose faces or features have been disfigured. May they – and we – never lose sight of their inner beauty.

Jesus would always go off some place to be alone and pray. Amidst all the rushing and pressure of life, may people take time to stop, to be alone with God, to find calm and peace.

12 JANUARY

John 3:22–30 ('he must grow greater')

Introduction to Mass
Baptism is a theme in today's gospel about John the Baptist. We pause for a moment to remember that our own baptism is 'now'. Now, we are blessed. Now, we are called.

Prayers of the Faithful
'He must grow greater, I must grow smaller.' We humbly put ourselves at the Lord's service. May all that we do be done for the glory of his name.

We give thanks to God for all those who put aside their own needs to think of another. We give thanks for all who work quietly in the background, seeking no reward.

Lent

ASH WEDNESDAY

Matthew 6:1–6, 16–18 (alms, prayer, fasting)

Introduction to Mass
The word 'Lent' refers to 'lengthening' – Springtime – the days getting longer. It is God offering us the feeling of things brightening up, a feeling of hope. Quietly, let us take God's offer into our hearts.

Prayers of the Faithful
Lent is about giving alms – may we find a practical way to express solidarity with the poor. Lent is about prayer – may we set aside a special quiet time each day. Lent is about fasting – may we practise self-restraint, in whatever way is most appropriate.

Let us pray for each other that our plans and hopes for Lent will bear fruit. Let us pause quietly, to offer to God the thing that we most want to happen during Lent.

THURSDAY AFTER ASH WEDNESDAY

Luke 9:22–25 ('if anyone wants to be a follower of mine')

Introduction to Mass
Lent is about choices we make, as today's readings teach us. We begin, though, by resting for a moment in the knowledge that, before any choice we make, God has already chosen us in Christ.

Prayers of the Faithful
At Lent we each ask ourselves, 'How can I be a follower of Christ in a better way than before?' May God's Spirit help us to discover practical ways in which we can become more faithful disciples.

At Lent Jesus invites us to save our lives, to find our very self. May that goal inspire us and attract us, as we follow through the choices we have made for Lent.

FRIDAY AFTER ASH WEDNESDAY

Matthew 9:14–15 ('and then they will fast')

Introduction to Mass
God's Word today is about fasting. Somebody said that the best kind of fasting is the fasting that frees us for something better. We think for a moment; what is the 'something better' I want to be freed for this Lent through my fasting?

Prayers of the Faithful
The gospel suggests that the disciples will fast when death takes Jesus away from them. We know that Jesus has conquered death and we await his return in glory. May our fasting increase our desire for his coming.

Isaiah says that the true kind of fasting is fasting from injustice and selfishness and uncaring. May this Lent see us grow in compassion, more committed to a more just and caring society.

SATURDAY AFTER ASH WEDNESDAY

Luke 5:27–32 (eating with tax-collectors and sinners)

Introduction to Mass
The Pharisees ask Jesus: 'Why do you eat and drink with sinners?' Here today, Jesus shares table with us, sinners in need of his mercy. We pause for a moment to feel his welcoming embrace.

Prayers of the Faithful
In eating with tax-collectors and sinners, Jesus shows the welcoming face of God. May we never despair of God's love for us. May we never think anyone is beyond the reach of God's love.

In the words of Isaiah, may we do away this Lent with the clenched fist and the wicked word. With the Lord's help, may we become more kind in what we say and what we do.

WEEK ONE – MONDAY

Matthew 25:31–46 (the sheep and goats)

Introduction to Mass
Today's readings tell us that we show our love for Christ in the way we treat one another. So we start our Mass by thinking of one another. Quietly we pray for those around us here and for all whom we'll meet today.

Prayers of the Faithful
The gospel talks of different needs – someone who needs food, someone who needs welcome, someone who needs a visit and support. We ask ourselves: who is waiting for my response today? Lord, inspire us to respond to others in need.

Other people see our faith in the way we live. May the love and concern we show in our lives attract others to Christ.

WEEK ONE – TUESDAY

Matthew 6:7–15 ('Our Father')

Introduction to Mass
In today's gospel, Jesus teaches his companions how to pray. He starts off by telling them not to babble on with many words! Let us heed his advice and begin our Mass with a moment of silent prayer.

Prayers of the Faithful
We thank God for this special prayer given to us by our Lord. We listen especially to Jesus' own emphasis on forgiveness. We pray that we will be willing to forgive others their failings.

May Lent be a special time of prayer for each of us, when we allow Jesus to teach us how to pray. May our prayer become deeper during this season.

WEEK ONE – WEDNESDAY

Luke 11:29–32 (the sign of Jonah)

Introduction to Mass
We hear in today's readings how the people of Nineveh repented when Jonah preached to them. We begin by asking God for the gift of repentance, and for the grace to change for the better.

Prayers of the Faithful
'There is something greater than Jonah here.' May this Lent be a time when we grow in our appreciation of who Jesus is – a time when we become more responsive to his call.

We thank God for other people around us who inspire us with the witness of their Christian lives. May we all encourage each other in Christian living.

WEEK ONE – THURSDAY

Matthew 7:7–12 ('ask and it will be given')

Introduction to Mass
Today's readings assure us that our God answers our prayers. So let us start by bringing our prayers before God, quietly calling on him to come to us in our need.

Prayers of the Faithful
We ask for the grace to be able to pray well. We ask God, who knows our need before ever we pray, to show us what to pray for.

When we pray, may we allow God to surprise us. May we be open to letting God answer our prayers in ways that we never expected.

WEEK ONE – FRIDAY

Matthew 5:20–26 ('be reconciled')

Introduction to Mass
The prophet Ezekiel tells us how much the Lord wants each of us to live – to renounce our sins and discover new life. May God's great concern for us encourage us now to repent.

Prayers of the Faithful
Jesus tells us to be reconciled before we come to the altar. Let us think of those we are having differences or difficulties with. Let us pray for a spirit of reconciliation.

Lord, grant each of us peace in our hearts. Help each of us to be a peaceful presence in the world. Help each of us to be a force for reconciliation.

WEEK ONE – SATURDAY

Matthew 5:43–48 ('love your enemies')

Introduction to Mass
Lent is a time of hope, of expectation, of new beginning. We begin our prayer by asking God to renew in our hearts the spirit of hope.

Prayers of the Faithful
God causes the sun to rise on bad people as well as good. May we come to see all people as God sees them, to see each person as God's beloved.

Somebody once said that my 'enemy' is simply the brother or sister I am estranged from. May all God's people learn to appreciate the dignity of those they are estranged from.

WEEK TWO – MONDAY

Luke 6:36–38 ('be compassionate')

Introduction to Mass
The spirit of today's gospel is the spirit of Christianity – gracious and generous, compassionate and understanding. So let us bathe ourselves in God's compassion – aware of our sins, but even more aware of God's loving mercy.

Prayers of the Faithful
We pray that we will treat others the way that God treats us – the way we want to be treated ourselves – with compassion and not judgment, with pardon and not condemnation.

May our Church be compassionate and not judgmental. We think of people who are on the margins. We think of people who feel excluded and not understood.

WEEK TWO – TUESDAY

Matthew 23:1–12 ('you have only one Teacher, the Christ')

Introduction to Mass
Our first reading from Isaiah is full of the spirit of Lent. 'Cease to do evil; learn to do good; search for justice – though your sins are like scarlet, they shall be white as snow'. In silence we ask the God of hope to fill our hearts with the spirit of repentance.

Prayers of the Faithful
Jesus tells us we are all equal as God's children. May none of us grow proud or think ourselves superior, or look down on any other person.

'Do not practise what they preach.' Jesus warns against hypocrisy. We pray especially for people who have leadership roles in our Church. Lord, grant them integrity. May they lead by example.

WEEK TWO – WEDNESDAY

Matthew 20:17–28 (the sons of Zebedee)

Introduction to Mass
Today Jesus says to his disciples, 'we are going up to Jerusalem'. Lent is our name for that journey; we travel the road with him. We open our hearts in prayer as we join Jesus on this road.

Prayers of the Faithful
'Can you drink the cup that I am going to drink?' May we join Jesus in his sacrifice. May we have a share of his spirit of self-giving. May we give ourselves generously to God and to others.

'The greatest among you must be your servant.' We pray for all who are involved in the parish and in the community. Protect us, Lord, from the temptations of power, status and privilege. Teach us the spirit of service and humility.

WEEK TWO – THURSDAY

Luke 16:19–31 (the rich man and Lazarus)

Introduction to Mass
If you put your trust in God, Jeremiah says, you're like a tree by the waterside, its roots drawing life from the stream. Let us pause and think of ourselves like that – our roots in God, drawing life and nourishment from Him.

Prayers of the Faithful
We pray for those among us like Lazarus – the poor, the struggling, the ignored. They are God's special ones. Grant us, Lord, some of your special love for the poor.

We pray from those among us like the rich man – those who are comfortable, who have more than enough. May they be humble and grateful. May they hear the cry of the poor.

WEEK TWO – FRIDAY

Matthew 21:33–43, 45–46 (the stone rejected by the builders)

Introduction to Mass
Today's gospel is about God's son being rejected and killed. It calls on us to take the opposite attitude, to welcome Jesus. So we pause quietly for a moment, with open hearts. We say to him: 'Come Lord Jesus.'

Prayers of the Faithful
There is a sense of shock in the gospel, at how God's own people can reject God's own gift. We pray for all in our Church, all God's people. May we always be amazed at what God gives to us.

We see envy and jealousy and hatred in today's readings. We pray for our own families and community, that they be filled with a spirit of kindness, and generosity of spirit, and mutual appreciation.

WEEK TWO – SATURDAY

Luke 15:1–3, 11–32 (the prodigal son)

Introduction to Mass
The theme of our readings is the boundless compassion of God. We begin with a quiet prayer of thanks to God, who understands us so well, and loves us with an everlasting love.

Prayers of the Faithful
The story leads us to pray for people who have strayed from the right path, or from God, or from the truth. This Lent, may they feel the attraction of God's open embrace, welcoming them home.

Jesus shows us the welcoming face of God. May our Christian community be, more and more, a place of welcome, where people can feel God's own welcoming embrace.

WEEK THREE – MONDAY

Luke 4:24–30 (no prophet is accepted in their own country)

Introduction to Mass
We begin our Mass by quietly repeating in our hearts the words of today's psalm: 'I will come to the altar of God, the God of my joy. My soul is thirsting for God, the God of my life'.

Prayers of the Faithful
The people are shocked and enraged at what Jesus says. We pray for ourselves, that our faith won't be too comfortable; that we will allow ourselves be surprised and challenged by what the Lord is saying.

The gospel tells us that Jesus is not sent to the Jews only. We pray that Christians will be open to appreciating God's Spirit at work in people who do not come to our Church or share our faith.

WEEK THREE – TUESDAY

Matthew 18:21–35 (how often must I forgive?)

Introduction to Mass
The theme today is forgiveness. We begin, as always, by celebrating God's forgiveness. We say in our hearts the words of the first reading: 'treat us gently, as you yourself are gentle and very merciful'.

Prayers of the Faithful
We know how hard it is to forgive. We pray for people who have been hurt by others and who are finding it difficult to forgive. We pray for God's peace for them.

May the Church we belong to be a place of forgiveness, inspired by God's own forgiving love. May people find the Church to be a place of mercy and acceptance.

WEEK THREE – WEDNESDAY

Matthew 5:17–19 ('not to abolish but to complete')

Introduction to Mass
In this third week of Lent, we begin our Mass by asking ourselves, 'How am I getting along, on my Lenten journey?' We ask God to encourage us and to renew our resolve.

Prayers of the Faithful
We pray now for one another, as we travel the journey of Lent. As we prepare for Easter, may each one here have a real sense of God's new life growing within us.

May the Christian community be a place of encouragement where people are inspired by the example of others to become more faithful followers of Christ.

WEEK THREE – THURSDAY

Luke 11:14–23 (the finger of God)

Introduction to Mass
Each day we pray, 'Thy kingdom come', and in today's gospel Jesus shows that God's kingdom is already among us, in his healings. Let us pray quietly in our hearts to God, 'Thy kingdom come'.

Prayers of the Faithful
We pray that we will be positive people, with hope-filled hearts. May we look for the signs of God's kingdom already among us, already happening in all kinds of ways.

In Jeremiah and in the psalm, the great sin is not listening, not paying attention. We think of the world we live in. We pray that people become more attentive to God and listen more seriously to God's Word.

WEEK THREE – FRIDAY

Mark 12:28–34 (love God; love your neighbour)

Introduction to Mass
Today's theme is Jesus' two great commandments: love God and love your neighbour. We turn to God in silent prayer: 'Lord, may your forgiveness release the love that is blocked in our hearts'.

Prayers of the Faithful
'With all your heart and all your soul and all your mind and all your strength.' May our love for God have that kind of energy and passion and enthusiasm and intensity.

'Love your neighbour as yourself.' May each of us be able to love ourselves and rejoice in our own beauty and accept ourselves as we are. May we give one another the same kind of love.

WEEK THREE – SATURDAY

Luke 18:9–14 (the Pharisee and the publican)

Introduction to Mass
Today's readings tell us to wait humbly for God. God will come to us, Hosea says, like spring rains watering the earth. We pray in our hearts: 'Come to us, our Lord and God'.

Prayers of the Faithful
The difference between the two people is that the Pharisee didn't ask God for anything; he didn't feel the need. May God protect us from being self-satisfied. May we always know our need of God, and turn to God in our need.

'People who prided themselves and despised everyone else.' We can only love others if we ourselves are humble. So we ask the Lord to teach us true humility and to never look down on others.

WEEK FOUR – MONDAY

John 4:43–54 (the court official's son)

Introduction to Mass
Lent is a time of new life, and in today's gospel we see the life-giving power of Jesus. Now, in a moment of quiet prayer, we open ourselves to Jesus' life-giving power.

Prayers of the Faithful
'The man believed what Jesus said and started on his way.' May our belief in Jesus support us on our way. May it give us courage and hope.

We think of sons and daughters who are sick or in any kind of distress. We think of their parents. We reach out to touch them with our prayers.

WEEK FOUR – TUESDAY

John 5:1–3, 5–16 (the man by the pool)

Introduction to Mass
Water is a big theme in the readings today. Water reminds us of our baptism. So we pause for a moment to give thanks for our baptism, the source of our new life in Christ.

Prayers of the Faithful
The man's illness had lasted thirty-eight years. We pray for those in our community who have been ill for a long time. We pray that they will have patience and hope, and the support of friends.

Jesus asks us the same question he asked the man by the pool: 'Do you want to be well again?' We pray that the desire in our heart will grow – our desire for new life; our desire to change for the better.

WEEK FOUR – WEDNESDAY

John 5:17–30 ('whoever believes has eternal life')

Introduction to Mass
Isaiah presents us with a powerful image of God. 'Can a mother forget the child of her womb? Even if she could, I will never forget you.' Let us rest for a moment to contemplate this God of ours.

Prayers of the Faithful
'Whoever believes in the one who sent me has passed from death to life.' It's a tremendous thought – we are already experiencing eternal life! Let us live our lives with gratitude and wonder.

In the words of Isaiah, the Lord consoles his people and takes pity on those who are afflicted. We think for a moment of people who are afflicted and we pray for God's consoling Spirit.

WEEK FOUR – THURSDAY

John 5:31–47 ('you refuse to accept me')

Introduction to Mass
The gospel says that we have never heard God's voice or seen God's shape. But now, in Jesus, God has a shape we can recognise and a voice we can hear. May our Eucharist today be a prayer of thanks for the face of God shown to us in Jesus.

Prayers of the Faithful
Jesus is speaking to us too, when he reproaches the people who do not believe, and who have no love of God in them, only interested in human approval. May this Lent challenge all Christians to a greater faith and a purer love.

In the first reading, we see the God of wrath give way to the God of mercy. We thank God for the journey we ourselves have travelled with our image of God. We pray for all who have yet to discover the God of love.

WEEK FOUR – FRIDAY

John 7:1–2, 10, 25–30 ('there is one who sent me')

Introduction to Mass
Lent is a time for coming to a deeper realisation of who Jesus is – the theme of today's gospel. We come into his presence now in silent prayer, he who is the Lord of our life.

Prayers of the Faithful
'There is one who sent me and I really come from him.' We pray that more people will be drawn to Jesus and captivated by him, and come to confess that he is the Christ.

In the first reading, godless people plan to torture the virtuous person. We give thanks for people who stand up for the truth and who point out wrongdoing, and who endure the suffering this may bring upon them.

WEEK FOUR – SATURDAY

John 7:40–52 ('there has never been anybody who spoke like this')

Introduction to Mass
The gospel today continues with the theme of the last few days – that of recognising who Jesus truly is. So, for a quiet moment, we each think about what he has come to mean for us

Prayers of the Faithful
'There has never been anybody who spoke like this.' The words carry a sense of surprise and amazement. We pray that, this Lent, each of us will be re-amazed by Jesus, in a new realisation of who he is.

Jeremiah describes himself as a sheep being led to the slaughter – words that anticipate what we will hear on Good Friday. We pray for people who suffer for their faith. May they draw strength and inspiration from Jesus.

WEEK FIVE – MONDAY

John 8:1–11 (the woman in adultery)
or
John 8:12–20 ('I am the light of the world')

Introduction to Mass
We are just a week and a half from the Easter Triduum. We pause for a moment before the Lord. We recall what we wanted from Lent. We reflect on how we have fared. We ask the Lord to give us new energy now.

Prayers of the Faithful
(If the gospel is John 8:1–11) – Those who condemned the woman saw only her past. But Jesus saw her future, her possibility. May this same Jesus encourage us to believe in ourselves and in what we can be.

(If the gospel is John 8:12–20) – 'I am the light of the world.' We thank Jesus, the light of our life, for enlightening our minds, for shining light on our path, for bringing light in our darkness.

Thinking of Susanna, we pray for people who are treated maliciously or accused falsely by others. We pray that all our relationships will be truthful and respectful.

WEEK FIVE – TUESDAY

John 8:21–30 ('I am from above')

Introduction to Mass
In today's psalm we hear: 'O Lord, listen to my prayer and let my cry for help reach you.' We stay quiet for a moment and think: What is my prayer to the Lord? What is my cry for help?

Prayers of the Faithful
The gospel ends with 'Many came to believe in him'. We pray for people who are searching, and for people who are struggling with their faith. May the Spirit guide them to Jesus.

As the days of Jesus' death and resurrection draw nearer, we pray that our faith will deepen, that we will appreciate more deeply that Jesus is the one sent by God.

WEEK FIVE – WEDNESDAY

John 8:31–42 ('the truth will make you free')

Introduction to Mass
Freedom is prominent in our gospel today. We come before the Lord in silence, and ask him to free us from whatever sin or weakness is enslaving or imprisoning us.

Prayers of the Faithful
We thank God for the freedom Jesus brought to many people in the gospels. We pray that we ourselves and many others will know his liberating power in our lives.

We pray for people who are not free, those who are prisoners of addiction, those who are in oppressive relationships, those who are trapped in despair. We pray for their freedom and their peace.

WEEK FIVE – THURSDAY

John 8:51–59 ('before Abraham was, I am')

Introduction to Mass
In the first reading, God makes a covenant with Abraham: 'I will be your God'. In the gospel we see that Jesus is the fulfilment of God's covenant. Quietly we thank God for coming close to us in love.

Prayers of the Faithful
In Jesus we have the complete expression of God's commitment to us. By the grace of God's Spirit, may our commitment in return grow firmer each day.

Jesus says, 'Whoever keeps my word will never see death'. We pray for our faithful departed, especially those whose faith has nourished our own faith. We thank God for them.

WEEK FIVE – FRIDAY

John 10:31–42 ('the Father is in me as I am in the Father')

Introduction to Mass
In the gospel readings this week, we see the opposition to Jesus mounting. Jesus says to the Jews: 'You refuse to believe in me'. We begin with a quiet moment, thanking God for our faith in his Son.

Prayers of the Faithful
'The Father is in me and I am in the Father.' Such a simple statement, yet it captures the essence of what Christians believe. May the truth of these words be rooted ever deeper in our hearts and minds.

Jeremiah, who endured opposition as Jesus did, says: 'I have committed my cause to the Lord.' We pray for Christians in difficult situations in different parts of the world. May God give them strength to endure opposition.

WEEK FIVE – SATURDAY

John 11:45–57 ('it is better for one man to die')

Introduction to Mass
The theme of today's Mass is unity – Jesus gathering into unity all the scattered children of God. This invites us, first of all, to appreciate our own unity, gathered here as God's family. We pause to give thanks.

Prayers of the Faithful
We pray for the unity of all God's people – for the unity of all Christians – for the unity of all faiths and religions. We pray for a spirit of mutual respect and appreciation.

The threat of death for Jesus is very real in this gospel. As we enter into Holy Week with him, we make this old Irish prayer our own: O King of the Friday, whose limbs were stretched on the cross; O Lord who did suffer the bruises, the wounds and the loss; we stretch ourselves beneath the shield of your might; some fruit from the tree of your passion fall on us this night.

HOLY WEEK – MONDAY

John 12:1–11 (Mary anoints Jesus' feet)

Introduction to Mass
We enter into Holy Week and the most sacred days of our year. We attend to Jesus, as Martha and Mary do in today's gospel. In silent prayer we give our hearts to him.

Prayers of the Faithful
Mary anoints the feet of Jesus. She ministers to him and cares for him and treasures him as death approaches. May we enter into that spirit and focus on what really matters this week.

God's words in Isaiah are words we apply to Jesus: 'Here is my chosen one, in whom my soul delights'. We apply the words to ourselves also. May we believe God saying to us: 'You are my chosen one; in you my soul delights'.

HOLY WEEK – TUESDAY

John 13:21–33, 36–38 ('one of you will betray me')

Introduction to Mass
Judas and Peter feature in today's gospel. As Jesus' death draws ever nearer, two of his companions betray him. It makes us mindful of our own weakness. Quietly we place our trust in the Lord's mercy and understanding.

Prayers of the Faithful
We see Judas betraying; we see Peter disowning; we see the other disciples wondering what's going on. We pray for ourselves. May the Lord strengthen our fragile faith and enlighten our muddied minds.

We think of people who have been betrayed by another. May they find peace in their hearts. We pray for people who have betrayed another. May they find hope in repentance.

HOLY WEEK – WEDNESDAY

Matthew 26:14–25 (Judas)

Introduction to Mass
The first reading and psalm are full of the mood of Good Friday – of Jesus' suffering, but also his confidence in God. For a moment of quiet we say nothing, but simply rest with him as he approaches death.

Prayers of the Faithful
We think of all the pain and suffering there is among us, in greater or lesser degree. We join our suffering with Jesus' suffering. We pray that we will experience in our lives the fruits of his suffering and death.

We pray for our Christian community, that the coming days will be a time of grace for all. We hope that many people will be touched in a new way by God's love for us in Christ.

HOLY THURSDAY

John 13:1–15 (Jesus washes his disciples' feet)

Introduction
We gather to praise God for the mystery that begins to unfold this evening. At the Last Supper, Jesus makes his death his great gift to us. We pause to contemplate God's self-giving, the source of our new life.

Prayers of the Faithful
May Jesus washing the feet of his disciples inspire us. May it teach us how to give, how to think of others often in life, how to keep the needs of others in mind.

We thank God for all the ways that people wash each other's feet, by thinking of each other and caring for one another. May our homes and neighbourhoods grow ever more thoughtful and caring.

Easter

EASTER MONDAY

Matthew 28:8–15 (awe and great joy)

Introduction to Mass
In our gospel, the women come from the tomb filled with awe and great joy. Those are our sentiments too as we celebrate the resurrection of Jesus – awe and great joy. We pause for a moment in quiet prayer.

Prayers of the Faithful
All this week's gospels are stories of the disciples encountering the risen Lord. And all the first readings are about their proclaiming the good news. May that be the pattern of our lives – experiencing the presence of the risen Jesus, and living our lives as a witness to the good news.

We celebrate the triumph of life over death. We celebrate hope. We pray for the people in our community, that many will know in their situation the new life and hope of Easter.

EASTER TUESDAY

John 20:11–18 (Mary of Magdala sees the Lord)

Introduction to Mass
In our gospel Mary of Magdala tells the disciples she has seen the Lord. We too have come to know the risen Lord in our lives. In the quiet of our hearts we praise God

Prayers of the Faithful
For Mary, weeping gives way to joy. We pray for all in our community who are weeping, feeling lost or desolate. May they know the joy of the risen Christ.

When people hear of the resurrection, they ask Peter 'what must we do?' and he says 'you must repent'. May the good news of the resurrection inspire us to turn away from sin and enter into the new life of Easter.

EASTER WEDNESDAY

Luke 24:13–35 (Emmaus)

Introduction to Mass
In our gospel story of the road to Emmaus, the disciples recognise Jesus in the breaking of bread. The 'breaking of bread' was the original name for the Eucharist. Now, in a moment of silence, we ready ourselves to recognise Jesus in the breaking of bread.

Prayers of the Faithful
May Jesus be our companion on the road of life, as he was for the two on the road to Emmaus. May he teach us about himself and open our eyes to recognise him. May he fill us with joy.

In Acts, we read of the transformation of the poor man at the Beautiful Gate. We think of ourselves and of others around us. We pray that lives will be transformed through the power of the risen Lord.

EASTER THURSDAY

Luke 24:35–48 ('peace be with you')

Introduction to Mass
The words that the risen Jesus said to the disciples, he now says to us: 'Peace be with you'. Let us rest for a moment in his peace and let us send a prayer to all gathered here, wishing peace to those around us.

Prayers of the Faithful
'Their joy was so great that they still could not believe it.' Lord, give us a share in that joy of the first disciples. May the good news of your resurrection bring joy to our eyes, to our hearts, to our lives.

Jesus asks: 'Why are there doubts rising in your hearts?' None of us is without questions and doubts. We pray for all who are struggling with their faith. May they know that God understands.

EASTER FRIDAY

John 21:1–14 (Jesus appears by the lake)

Introduction to Mass
In our gospel, the risen Jesus appears by the lake and breaks bread with his disciples. And here too, in our gathering, he comes among us in the breaking of bread. We say in our hearts, 'Come Lord Jesus'.

Prayers of the Faithful
'They knew quite well it was the Lord.' We pray for the gift of recognition – to be able to recognise him present in all kinds of different situations through the day.

In the first reading, we can feel Peter's confidence and gladness in telling people about Jesus' rising. Lord, give all baptised Christians a share of that gladness, and that confidence to tell the world about Christ.

EASTER SATURDAY

Mark 16:9–15 ('go out to the whole world')

Introduction to Mass
Once again today, our readings are about the good news of the resurrection. Let us begin with a quiet prayer of thanks, that we are graced to know the good news.

Prayers of the Faithful
Three times in the gospel today, we hear of Jesus' former companions not believing he was risen. May we take comfort from this. May the Spirit help us in our disbelief and help all who find it hard to believe.

'Proclaim the good news to all creation.' We are all witnesses; we are all called. May we share good news by the way we live our lives – with joy and hope and love.

WEEK TWO – MONDAY

John 3:1–8 ('you must be born from above')

Introduction to Mass
Easter means new life, new hope, new beginnings. And so, in the silence of our hearts, we bring before the Lord our own need to be renewed, our desire to be made new.

Prayers of the Faithful
Jesus says, 'you must be born from above'. This is the new life of faith, of baptism, lived in the power of the Spirit. We pray for the power of the Spirit to renew and transform the life of our Christian community.

In the reading from Acts, they were all filled with the Holy Spirit and began to proclaim the word of God boldly. May the same Spirit give us courage to proclaim the gospel in our words and in our actions.

WEEK TWO – TUESDAY

John 3:7–15 ('the wind blows where it pleases')

Introduction to Mass
Today's gospel message overlaps with yesterday's: 'you must be born from above'. We reflect for a moment on our baptism, our new life in Christ. We thank God for the new life of Easter flowing through us.

Prayers of the Faithful
'The whole group of believers was united heart and soul.' We pray that our Christian community may be like this, animated by a single spirit. We make the same prayer for all Christian communities.

'None was ever in want.' We pray that our Christian community will have the same spirit of solidarity. May we become more aware of the needs around us, more sensitive and more responsive.

WEEK TWO – WEDNESDAY

John 3:16–21 ('God loves the world so much')

Introduction to Mass
'No one who believes in Jesus will be condemned.' Let us take heart from the words of today's gospel. Let us approach the Lord with our faith, confident of his enduring love and mercy.

Prayers of the Faithful
'God loves the world so much.' We are united here in our appreciation of God's inexpressible love. We think of people who do not, or cannot believe in that love. May God's love flood their hearts.

'God loves the world so much.' We think of this world that God loves so much. May it develop into the kind of world God wants it to be, with more compassion and less suffering, more solidarity and less division.

WEEK TWO – THURSDAY

John 3:31–36 ('the Father loves the Son')

Introduction to Mass
The resurrection reveals to us that Jesus is God's beloved Son. We offer God a quiet prayer of praise, for sharing God's very life with us.

Prayers of the Faithful
Today's readings are about those who do, and those who don't, recognise who Jesus is. We pray that the Spirit will work in people's hearts, drawing them to confess that Jesus is the Son of God.

'He whom God has sent speaks God's own words.' We think of people who have been like Christ to us – people who have put us in touch with God and God's own words. May God bless them.

WEEK TWO – FRIDAY

John 6:1–15 (the loaves and fishes)

Introduction to Mass
In our gospel, a small boy brings five loaves and two fishes to Jesus. Now in our Eucharist we bring everything to God. However little it may seem, we bring it now to God.

Prayers of the Faithful
May we all feel the miracle of God's presence. May we realise how much God is doing when we seem to have so little. May we trust ourselves to God.

Thinking of the feeding, we pray for parents as they feed their families. We pray for those who bring food to the housebound. We pray for those who feed the hungry and the homeless.

WEEK TWO – SATURDAY

John 6:16–21 (Jesus walking on the lake)

Introduction to Mass
In the gospel, Jesus comes to the disciples, struggling on the stormy lake. We pause now to feel Jesus' presence with us, in whatever difficulties we are going through.

Prayers of the Faithful
'It is I, do not be afraid.' We pray for any among us who are afraid, whatever their fear may be. May they hear Jesus speaking these words to them. May they begin to feel his peace.

In the first reading, the seven chosen are the origins of deacons in our Church. So we pray for deacons working in our parishes. May they mirror to each one of us our own call to serve and to help in the community.

WEEK THREE – MONDAY

John 6:22–29 ('look for food that endures')

Introduction to Mass
Our gospel readings this week are all about Jesus the bread of life. So, at the start of the week, we open ourselves in our need to be nourished by Jesus the bread of life.

Prayers of the Faithful
Jesus tells the crowd that what they came looking for, and what he is offering, may not be the same thing. May we learn from this, to put aside our little needs, and ask Jesus to put us in touch with our deepest needs.

Stephen is inspired by the Holy Spirit, but is met with opposition and false accusations. We pray that all Christians have the same courage and inspiration to witness to what they believe.

WEEK THREE – TUESDAY

John 6:30–35 ('I am the bread of life')

Introduction to Mass
Jesus, the bread of life, says to us, 'Whoever comes to me will never be hungry'. Quietly now, we bring before him our hunger, our thirst, our faith.

Prayers of the Faithful
Jesus is the bread that gives life to the world. We pray for all who are searching for new life, for hope. We wish for them all the new life that Jesus can give them.

As Stephen is being stoned, he says, 'Lord Jesus, receive my spirit'. We pray for all who are dying around now. May they have the same trust as Stephen to place themselves in the Lord's power.

WEEK THREE – WEDNESDAY

John 6:35–40 ('I am the bread of life')

Introduction to Mass
Again in today's gospel Jesus says, 'I am the bread of life'. Let us pause a moment to hear his invitation sounding in our hearts – his love for us, his life-giving presence within us and among us.

Prayers of the Faithful
'Whoever comes to me, I shall not turn away.' We think of people who feel unworthy to come, or unwelcome. We ask God to give us a welcoming spirit. May others find God's welcome in our welcome.

Saul worked for the total destruction of the Church. We pray for people who are gripped by a spirit of destruction. May God's gentle, healing spirit give them freedom and peace.

WEEK THREE – THURSDAY

John 6:44–51 ('I am the living bread')

Introduction to Mass
Jesus says, 'No one can come to me unless they are drawn by the Father'. We are gathered here because each of us has been drawn by the Father to Jesus. We rest for a moment in that grace.

Prayers of the Faithful
'Whoever eats this bread will live for ever.' We thank God for this daily miracle of the bread of heaven. We thank the Lord, who gives us each day our daily bread.

The Ethiopian in the first reading went on his way rejoicing after his baptism. May all of us be awakened to a new awareness of our baptism. May all Christians learn to rejoice.

WEEK THREE – FRIDAY

John 6:52–59 ('my flesh is real food')

Introduction to Mass
Jesus says, 'Whoever eats me will draw life from me.' We come together before the table of the Lord, to draw life from him, who is the source of our life. We pray quietly for a moment.

Prayers of the Faithful
We share in common the bread of life – the life of the risen Christ. We are already living a life divine. May we live our lives with gratitude and hope.

Today Saul is baptised, as the Ethiopian was in yesterday's reading. This Easter season is a time for remembering our baptism. May we all carry our baptism in our hearts each day.

WEEK THREE – SATURDAY

John 6:60–69 ('who shall we go to?')

Introduction to Mass
Jesus says to Peter, do you want to go away too? Peter says, where would we go? You have the message of eternal life. In the quiet of our hearts we say with Peter: 'We know you are the Holy One of God'.

Prayers of the Faithful
We say a prayer of thanks for the enrichment of this week's gospel readings, about Jesus the bread of life. As we receive this bread, may we also become the bread of life for others around us.

We make the words of today's first reading a prayer for our community, and for all our neighbouring Christian communities – May we live in peace, building ourselves up, living in the fear of the Lord and filled with the consolation of the Holy Spirit.

WEEK FOUR – MONDAY

John 10:11–18 (good shepherd) – year A

John 10:1–10 ('I have come that they may have life') – years B and C

Introduction to Mass
(Year A): Jesus says, 'I am the good shepherd'. For us Christians, this is one of our greatest images for God's care of us. We rest a moment in the knowledge of God's care.

(Years B and C): Jesus says in today's gospel, I have come so that you may have life, and have it to the full. In quiet prayer let us embrace his Easter gift in our hearts – this invitation, this possibility of fulness of life.

Prayers of the Faithful
(Year A): We praise God for Jesus who lays down his life for us, for Jesus who knows us, for Jesus who leads us into new places.

(Years B and C): We make our own the words of Jesus today. May we know his voice. May we be safe. May we know freedom in his care. May we find pasture. May we have fulness of life.

(All Years): Our first reading is about the first disciples realising that God's love in Christ is meant for all of humanity. We praise God for the variety of ways people find God, in different faiths and different religions.

WEEK FOUR – TUESDAY

John 10:22–30 ('the Father and I are one')

Introduction to Mass
The first reading tells us it was at Antioch that the disciples were first called 'Christians'. We rest for a moment in quiet appreciation of the dignity and privilege of this, our Easter calling; we are 'Christians'.

Prayers of the Faithful
'The sheep that belong to me listen to my voice.' We thank God for the belonging we feel in the presence of Jesus. We pray that many more people will know the joy of belonging.

We listen again to the words said of Barnabas in the first reading; we make them a prayer for ourselves and for all whom we know – a good person, filled with the Holy Spirit and with faith.

WEEK FOUR – WEDNESDAY

John 12:44–50 (I, the light)

Introduction to Mass
Jesus says, 'Whoever sees me, sees the one who sent me'. This is the heart of our faith – in Jesus we see God. So we rest a moment with these words: 'Whoever sees me, sees the one who sent me'.

Prayers of the Faithful
Jesus is the light; people need not stay in the darkness anymore. For ourselves and others we pray, to be led out of our darkness, to allow ourselves be drawn to the light.

Jesus says he came, not to condemn, but to save. We pray for people who think they are condemned – people who have been judged and rejected by others – and people who have condemned themselves. May the light of salvation break through the darkness.

WEEK FOUR – THURSDAY

John 13:16–20 ('whoever welcomes the one I send')

Introduction to Mass
We find the theme of welcome in today's gospel. So it's appropriate to begin with welcome. Let all who are gathered here feel God's welcome, God's welcoming embrace for each one of us. We pause to be quiet.

Prayers of the Faithful
'Whoever welcomes the one I send welcomes me.' We pray for all in our community who reach out to others in the name of Jesus. May they be welcomed, wherever they go. May others come closer to Jesus through them.

'Whoever welcomes me welcomes the one who sent me.' May people discover more and more the fulness of who Jesus is – not just an inspirational human being – but the very presence of God among us.

WEEK FOUR – FRIDAY

John 14:1–6 ('I am the way, the truth and the life')

Introduction to Mass
Let us take some phrases from the readings as our introductory thought today. Listen to these words and rest with them a moment. 'We are here to tell you the good news.' 'Jesus is the way, the truth and the life.' 'This message of salvation is meant for you.'

Prayers of the Faithful
'Do not let your hearts be troubled.' We pray for all with troubled hearts – among us here, and elsewhere. Jesus encourages us to trust in him. May all with troubled hearts rest in him and find peace in him.

'I am going to prepare a place for you.' We pray for our dead – all those we have known over the years. We rejoice in Jesus, who has gone ahead of them to greet them.

EASTER

WEEK FOUR – SATURDAY

John 14:7–14 ('to have seen me is to have seen the Father')

Introduction to Mass
Again in today's gospel we hear expressed the core of what we believe – 'to have seen me is to have seen the Father'. We make a quiet prayer of praise and thanks, that in Jesus the face of God is revealed to us.

Prayers of the Faithful
We put ourselves in the shoes of Philip, as Jesus says, 'Have I been with you all this time, Philip, and you still do not know me?' May we be humble and ready to learn. May God's Spirit help us to know Jesus more deeply.

'If you ask for anything in my name, I will do it.' We quietly bring our own needs to mind. We become aware of the deepest prayers within us. Confidently, we bring them to Jesus.

WEEK FIVE – MONDAY

John 14:21–26 (Jesus makes his home with us)

Introduction to Mass
Listen to Jesus' words today to all who follow him; I and the Father will come to you and make our home with you. We know he has made his home in our hearts. Now we open our hearts to him, to receive him once more.

Prayers of the Faithful
'The Holy Spirit will teach you and remind you of all that I've said.' We ask for a listening heart – to be led by the Spirit, to learn and be attentive, to grow both wise and humble.

In the first reading, a man who had never walked is healed. We think of similar people in our society. We pray for all who have been disabled or paralysed. We pray for the gift of divine courage.

WEEK FIVE – TUESDAY

John 14:27–31 ('peace I give you')

Introduction to Mass
Jesus' words today speak to a deep need in all of us. So let us take his words into our hearts and into our need. He says, Peace I give you; my own peace I give you.

Prayers of the Faithful
We reach out in our prayer to people who are crying out for peace, for peace in a relationship, for inner, heartfelt peace, for peace amidst community strife.

In the first reading, Barnabas and Paul 'put fresh heart into the disciples, encouraging them to persevere in the faith'. We make this our prayer for all whose faith is tested. Lord, put fresh heart into your disciples.

WEEK FIVE – WEDNESDAY

John 15:1–8 ('I am the vine')

Introduction to Mass
'I am the vine; you are the branches.' We are attached to Jesus. His life flows into us and out from us. We rest a moment with this thought. We feel ourselves rooted in him.

Prayers of the Faithful
'Make your home in me.' May we make our home in Jesus. May we listen to his word. May our lives bear fruit in a love that is real and active.

'You are the branches.' We are all interconnected, as branches of the vine. We pray now with love for people we know who are suffering in any way.

WEEK FIVE – THURSDAY

John 15:9–11 ('remain in my love')

Introduction to Mass
In today's gospel, Jesus says simply, 'Remain in my love'. We stay quietly for a moment with that thought – remaining in his love – the love that fills our hearts – that carries and sustains us each day.

Prayers of the Faithful
'So that my joy may be in you and your joy be complete.' May there be joy in all hearts, whatever our situation, knowing that we remain in Jesus' love. May there be joy on our faces, so that the hearts of others will be lifted up.

The first reading is about the most momentous time for the early Christians – their seeing that the good news was for everybody, not just Jews. We pray for all God's people, for all of us live in the shadow of God's love.

WEEK FIVE – FRIDAY

John 15:12–17 (love one another)

Introduction to Mass
'Love one another' is the message of today's gospel. It is followed by Jesus saying, I do not call you servants, I call you friends. We reflect for a moment on what we are – not servants, but friends of Jesus.

Prayers of the Faithful
'Love one another as I have loved you.' This is Christian living at its most simple and its most profound. We pray that we will be loving people, inspired by what Jesus' love for us means to us.

We pray for the people who love us, including those gone before us. We thank God for them; they show us that Jesus calls us to love, just as we have been loved.

WEEK FIVE – SATURDAY

John 15:18–21 ('you do not belong to the world')

Introduction to Mass
Today Jesus says to us: 'You do not belong to the world'. He is reminding us of the life God has destined us for. We pause for a moment with thankful hearts.

Prayers of the Faithful
'You do not belong to the world.' Our Christian community is a 'home from home'. May all in our community feel they belong, feel at home. May this give us a foretaste of our eternal home, where we belong with God.

Jesus says the world may hate you. Our loyalty lies elsewhere, in the kingdom of God. Even so, may this give us a love and loyalty for God's world and God's people. May we help build God's kingdom today.

WEEK SIX – MONDAY

John 15:26–16:4 (the Spirit of truth)

Introduction to Mass
The gospel for the next few days is about the Holy Spirit – reminding us that Pentecost is near. We begin by opening ourselves once more to the gift of God's Spirit.

Prayers of the Faithful
The Spirit unites us to Jesus, and is the pledge of God's undying love for us. We give thanks for the gift of God's Holy Spirit. In the power of the Spirit, may we make ourselves a gift to others.

'I have told you all this so that your faith may not be shaken.' We pray for those whose faith is fragile or shaken or threatened. May God's Spirit support them and give them security.

WEEK SIX – TUESDAY

John 16:5–11 ('I will send the Advocate')

Introduction to Mass
Jesus' gift of the Spirit unites us all here as one. We pause to become aware of the Spirit amongst us, the Spirit of our gathering, the Spirit in one another.

Prayers of the Faithful
We have received the Spirit. May the Spirit of Jesus inspire us in Christian living. May we bear the fruits of the Spirit, in our kindness, our truthfulness, our love.

In the first reading, the whole family is converted and baptised. We pray for all the families in our community. May their homes be places where each person enters into the joy of baptism.

WEEK SIX – WEDNESDAY

John 16:12–15 (the Spirit of truth will lead you)

Introduction to Mass
Paul says: God is not far from any one – in God, we live and move and exist. Let us be quiet for a moment in the presence of our God, who is not far from any one of us here.

Prayers of the Faithful
'The Spirit will lead you to the complete truth.' We pray that this will be our experience. May the Spirit lead us to the light – to a deeper understanding of God, of life, of ourselves.

Like Athens in the first reading, the good news of the gospel has become unfamiliar to many in our society. We pray for Christians who, like Paul, seek to communicate the gospel in this world.

WEEK SIX – THURSDAY

John 16:16–20 (your sorrow will turn to joy)

Introduction to Mass
Our gospel is about presence and absence – Jesus leaving and returning again. So we begin by quietly rejoicing at his presence among us – and at the joy this brings to us.

Prayers of the Faithful
'Your sorrow will turn to joy.' We think of people we know who are sorrowful or weeping. We pray for them, knowing that Christ's presence brings a joy to us even when we are filled with sorrow.

From the first reading, our prayer is for all who seek to communicate the good news of the gospel in our community. May they share some of Paul's spirit of eloquence and persuasiveness.

WEEK SIX – FRIDAY

John 16:20–23 (your hearts will be full of joy)

Introduction to Mass
Again, today's gospel is about joy. Our Christian faith is a thing of joy. Let us reflect for a moment on the joy that it brings us.

Prayers of the Faithful
The image in our gospel invites us to pray for all women giving birth – and also for all others who are enduring pain or suffering for the sake of a greater joy. May we all give of ourselves, and increase the joy in the world.

Jesus gives us a joy that no one can take from us. May that joy be evident in what we say and what we do. May it be visible on our faces! May we radiate joy and hope.

WEEK SIX – SATURDAY

John 16:23–28 (the Father loves you for loving me)

Introduction to Mass
Jesus says, the Father loves you for loving me. Let us stay with that thought for a moment – we are part of a circle of love reaching into God. Jesus says to us, the Father loves you for loving me.

Prayers of the Faithful
'Ask and you will receive.' God knows what we truly and most deeply need. So we ask God to help us pray; to lead us in our prayer to our deepest desires.

'Ask and you shall receive.' We each think now of somebody we would like to pray for. We think of our wishes and hopes for that person. We bless them with our prayer.

WEEK SEVEN – MONDAY

John 16:29–33 ('be brave')

Introduction to Mass
Jesus says, In the world you will have trouble, but you will have peace in me. Let us now bring our troubles before him – and allow his peace to descend upon us in this Eucharist.

Prayers of the Faithful
'In the world you will have trouble, but you will have peace in me.' We pray for people we know who are troubled. May all who are troubled hear Jesus' words: 'be brave, I have conquered the world'.

In the first reading, people say to Paul, 'we were never told there was such a thing as the Holy Spirit'. In these days leading up to Pentecost, may we come to a new awareness and appreciation of God's Holy Spirit.

WEEK SEVEN – TUESDAY

John 17:1–11 ('I pray for them')

Introduction to Mass
Jesus says to the Father, 'I pray for them'. Let us stay with this thought for a moment. Jesus, seated at the right hand of the Father, is praying for us. Let us enter quietly into his prayer.

Prayers of the Faithful
'Eternal life is this, to know you, the only true God.' We know that God is in every heart. We pray that everyone may know in their heart the life-giving God within them.

Paul describes his mission in our first reading. We make his words our own. May we carry out the mission the Lord Jesus gave us, to bear witness to the good news of God's grace.

WEEK SEVEN – WEDNESDAY

John 17:11–19 ('consecrate them in the truth')

Introduction to Mass
Again today's gospel sees Jesus praying for us to the Father. Let us be quiet for a moment and imagine we are listening in! What might be Jesus' prayer for me?

Prayers of the Faithful
Let us listen again to what Jesus prays for us: 'May they be one.' 'Protect them from the evil one.' 'Consecrate them in the truth.' We make his prayer our prayer.

In the first reading, Paul quotes Jesus as saying, 'there is more happiness in giving than in receiving.' May we learn to be generous givers, thinking of others often in life. May we also be gracious in receiving.

WEEK SEVEN – THURSDAY

John 17:20–26 ('may they all be one')

Introduction to Mass
For three days now in the gospel, Jesus is praying for us. His prayer today is for unity. We contemplate quietly for a moment how we are all one in God's eyes and in God's love.

Prayers of the Faithful
'May they be so completely one.' May God's love flow through us and unite us. May all Christians realise their deep unity in Christ. May all humanity realise its deep unity in God.

Jesus prays that the love with which the Father loves him may be in us. The Father loves us with the same love as for Jesus. Let our hearts be amazed as we give thanks and praise.

WEEK SEVEN – FRIDAY

John 21:15–19 ('do you love me?')

Introduction to Mass
Jesus asks Peter: 'Do you love me?' Peter says: 'Yes Lord, you know that I love you'. In our hearts we now have the same conversation. We hear Jesus asking, 'Do you love me?' We hear ourselves saying in reply, 'Yes Lord, you know that I love you'.

Prayers of the Faithful
Peter's threefold denial of Jesus is superseded by his threefold 'I love you'. As each of us, like Peter, says to Jesus, 'I love you', may we feel healing of our betrayals and a new oneness with him.

Let us, with Peter, stretch out our hand. Let us allow Jesus lead us where he wants to bring us. May we trust him and follow him.

WEEK SEVEN – SATURDAY

John 21:20–25 ('you are to follow me')

Introduction to Mass
Jesus says to Peter: Don't worry about anybody else – you are to follow me. For a quiet moment we focus our minds on this. Our life's work, our life's task, is to follow him.

Prayers of the Faithful
For six weeks now we have been listening each day to John's gospel. We praise God for this wonderful gift, and for how it has enriched and enhanced our faith.

We thank God for the Easter season now completed. We thank God for the new life and hope it has brought. On the eve of Pentecost, we pray for a new descent of God's Spirit in the Church and in the world.

Ordinary Time

WEEK ONE – MONDAY

Mark 1:14–20 ('Believe the good news'; 'follow me')

Introduction to Mass
Jesus speaks the first words of his ministry in today's gospel and he calls his first disciples. We quietly turn to him now, to hear his words and to hear his call.

Prayers of the Faithful
Jesus' first words are about good news. May the good news of God's love fill our hearts. May we live our Christian lives in a mood of joy and of hope. And may we bring this spirit to bear on everything.

Jesus calls his first disciples. He calls each one of us too, though we may fail to appreciate it. Let us live our Christian calling with energy and generosity. May we respond as readily as the first disciples did.

WEEK ONE – TUESDAY

Mark 1:21–28 (he teaches with authority; unclean spirit)

Introduction to Mass
Jesus' teaching made a deep impression on the people. Let us pause a moment to reflect with gratitude on the deep impression he has made on us.

Prayers of the Faithful
May this power of Jesus free us from anything within that is dominating or oppressing us. We make the same prayer for others who are in the power of evil or negative forces.

This gospel says twice that Jesus teaches with authority. May we listen seriously and intently to everything Jesus says, knowing that he is the Word of God.

WEEK ONE – WEDNESDAY

Mark 1:29–39 (Jesus heals many; he goes off to pray)

Introduction to Mass
We see Jesus' healing power in today's gospel. As we begin our Mass we come before him in our own need of healing, trusting in his power.

Prayers of the Faithful
So many who crowded around Jesus; so many whom he healed. We open our hearts to all the suffering in our world, and in people we know. We pray for the power of Jesus' compassion in ourselves and in our world.

Jesus went off alone to pray. May prayer be the heartbeat of our lives too, the source from which our compassion flows.

WEEK ONE – THURSDAY

Mark 1:40–45 (Jesus heals a leper)

Introduction to Mass
In our gospel, Jesus says to the leper: 'Of course I want to heal you'. We listen now to Jesus saying those same words to us: 'Of course I want to heal you'.

Prayers of the Faithful
We put ourselves in the place of the leper. We pray for all among us who suffer from any kind of skin disease. We pray for anybody who is shunned because of their appearance or their infirmity.

We make ourselves aware of how Jesus feels for each of us. We thank God for the healing we have known at different times in our life. May this help us live our lives with gratitude.

ORDINARY TIME

WEEK ONE – FRIDAY

Mark 2:1–12 (Jesus heals a paralytic)

Introduction to Mass
Jesus says to the paralysed man, 'your sins are forgiven'. Let us feel the burden being lifted as Jesus says to us too, 'your sins are forgiven'.

Prayers of the Faithful
We think of people who are paralysed or who are not as mobile as they used to be. We think of the people who support and carry them.

Four people carried the paralysed man to Jesus. We think of people who have carried us, or who are carrying and supporting us now. We think too of people whom we ourselves are carrying and supporting.

WEEK ONE – SATURDAY

Mark 2:13–17 (Jesus' table fellowship)

Introduction to Mass
Today we see Jesus sharing table with tax-collectors and sinners. And here today, he shares table with us. Let us pause to accept his hospitality and to thank him for accepting us as we are.

Prayers of the Faithful
This is one of Jesus' most characteristic actions, sharing a table with outcasts and sinners. We rejoice in this, the face of our welcoming God, who includes everybody, who brings people in from the cold.

May we ourselves be the welcoming face of God. May we spread Jesus' hospitality, his inclusive welcoming spirit.

WEEK TWO – MONDAY

Mark 2:18–22 (new wineskins)

Introduction to Mass
There's a theme of newness in today's gospel. Jesus brings something new into our lives. We live new lives in him. Let us pray for a moment for a new spirit, a new heart, a new beginning.

Prayers of the Faithful
Jesus' disciples not fasting tells us something about the new mood of joy there was in his presence. We do practise fasting, but our predominant mood as Christians is one of joy. May our being in Jesus' presence make us joyful.

'New wine, new wineskins'. May our faith feel new and fresh, not old or stale. Lord, help us to let go of what is holding us back, what is no longer of service – so that we can embrace the new.

WEEK TWO – TUESDAY

Mark 2:23–28 (master of the Sabbath)

Introduction to Mass
Today's gospel invites us to see Jesus as a free spirit who wants us to be free as well. We come to him now and ask him to free us of what is weighing us down, blocking or frustrating us.

Prayers of the Faithful
In the last four days' gospels, religious leaders have disputed with Jesus over his practices – forgiving, eating with outcasts, his disciples not fasting, ignoring Sabbath observances. May Jesus challenge us to focus on the heart of true religion that underlies all rules and rituals and observances.

Jesus is master of the Sabbath. We pray that our Sunday celebrations will help people to connect with Jesus our Lord and be nourished by him.

WEEK TWO – WEDNESDAY

Mark 3:1–6 (man with withered hand)

Introduction to Mass
Jesus says to the man whom he heals: 'Stretch out your hand'. He reaches out to us too, and we reach out to him. We pause for a moment, to feel his healing touch.

Prayers of the Faithful
We thank God for the gift of our hands. We think of people who are deprived in any way of the use of their hands.

Jesus is telling those who were watching that religion can have the effect of blinding its followers to human need. May we take his words to heart. May we who are in touch with Jesus share his boundless compassion for all who are in pain.

WEEK TWO – THURSDAY

Mark 3:7–12 (crowding forward to touch him)

Introduction to Mass
We hear in the gospel the unclean spirits shouting to Jesus, 'You are the Son of God'. We begin with a quiet prayer of adoration as we say in our hearts, 'You are the Son of God'.

Prayers of the Faithful
'Great numbers heard of all that he was doing.' We hope that it may be so today, that many people will hear of Jesus and be drawn to him. May we help that come about, through the witness of our Christian lives.

'So many were crowding forward to touch him.' So many people are crying out for help. So many are searching for healing. With Jesus' compassion in our hearts, we reach out to them in our prayer.

WEEK TWO – FRIDAY

Mark 3:13–19 (calling the twelve)

Introduction to Mass
Today's gospel begins: 'Jesus summoned those he wanted'. Reflect quietly for a moment. He summons me; he wants me.

Prayers of the Faithful
Jesus called the twelve who were to be his companions. This tells us that he does not work alone. He makes others partners in his work, his mission. Lord, we thank you for calling us to be your co-workers.

One by one, we hear the names of the twelve. The Lord calls each person by name. May each of us hear him call us by name. May we rejoice as we discover the part we have to play.

WEEK TWO – SATURDAY

Mark 3:20–21 ('out of his mind')

Introduction to Mass
We open our hearts to God as we begin our Mass. In the quiet of our hearts we open ourselves to God, who loves us with an infinite love.

Prayers of the Faithful
Some people barely get time to breathe, with all the demands that others put on them. We ask God to bless them. We think of people of whom we demand a lot. And we pray that we will be patient and kind when others make demands on us.

'They were convinced he was out of his mind.' We thank God for this insight into the impression Jesus made on people close to him. We thank God for the sense it gives of Jesus' passion and energy. May we allow Jesus to surprise us with who he really is.

WEEK THREE – MONDAY

Mark 3:22–30 (Beelzebul, sin against Spirit)

Introduction to Mass
Through the power of God, Jesus casts out devils. Let us begin with a quiet prayer, asking him to free us from the forces of sin and evil that oppress us.

Prayers of the Faithful
This gospel is about recognising Jesus and where he comes from. We pray that many people will be drawn by his words and attracted by his deeds – that many will recognise in him the power and presence of God.

Jesus talks about the sin that cannot be forgiven. We know God's forgiveness has no bounds, so perhaps the unforgiveable sin is when we don't allow ourselves to be forgiven. We pray that nobody will shut themselves off from God's forgiving love in Christ.

WEEK THREE – TUESDAY

Mark 3:31–35 ('my brother and sister and mother')

Introduction to Mass
Jesus says, anyone who does the will of God is his brother and sister and mother. Let us think quietly for a moment, how intimately we are related to Jesus – each one of us as close to him as family.

Prayers of the Faithful
St Augustine said that we are all called to be mothers of Christ – not in the sense of giving birth to him physically, but in a spiritual sense. May we each, like Mary, say 'Yes' to him in our hearts and allow his life to grow within us.

What matters, says Jesus, is to do the will of God – to 'walk the talk'. May we put our faith into action, so that our lives are an eloquent expression of what we believe.

WEEK THREE – WEDNESDAY

Mark 4:1–20 (the sower)

Introduction to Mass
We hear today the parable of the sower. The story invites us to open our hearts, to welcome the Word, to be receptive. We pray quietly for a moment.

Prayers of the Faithful
The good news of the gospel is the seed. Our hearts are the soil. May our hearts be good soil, welcoming and receptive. May the joy and hope of the gospel grow in our hearts.

We think of the obstacles Jesus speaks of. We pray for people (ourselves included) who are prevented from hearing the good news – by tribulations, by worries or by the lure of material things.

WEEK THREE – THURSDAY

Mark 4:21–25 (the lamp, the measure)

Introduction to Mass
Jesus says today, 'the amount you measure out is the amount you will be given'. In that spirit, we ask the Lord to forgive our wrongs and shortcomings. And we pray that we will be forgiving of others in the same measure.

Prayers of the Faithful
With the image of the lamp, Jesus speaks to each of us. May we let our faith shine through in our lives. May our faith be confident.

With the image of the lamp, Jesus speaks to us collectively as a Christian community. May we not keep our Christianity hidden in our Churches. May we reach out. May the amount we reach out be the amount we are enriched.

WEEK THREE – FRIDAY

Mark 4:26–34 (parables of seeds)

Introduction to Mass
Jesus today tells us parables about seeds and growth. We begin our Eucharist with a silent prayer of thanks, for how our faith and hope have grown, for the seed of God's love planted in our hearts.

Prayers of the Faithful
In the first parable Jesus likens the kingdom to a seed that grows away mysteriously. We ask God to give us trust – as well as eyes to see how God is at work in our lives, bringing growth in surprising, mysterious ways.

Listening to the parable of the mustard seed, we pray for people who are trying to begin again, and for people who feel they have a mountain to climb. We pray that they will take the first small steps, that they will trust in the power of small beginnings – the power of the Spirit.

WEEK THREE – SATURDAY

Mark 4:35–41 (calming the storm)

Introduction to Mass
In today's gospel Jesus calms the storm. The story speaks powerfully to us. Let us hear Jesus, amidst our own tribulations, speaking the same words to us: 'Quiet now! Be calm!'

Prayers of the Faithful
We pray for people we know who are going through troubled times. May the Lord be with them as a calming presence.

We pray for ourselves. May Jesus be with us when things are difficult. May our faith be stronger than our fear.

WEEK FOUR – MONDAY

Mark 5:1–20 (unclean spirits)

Introduction to Mass
Jesus heals a man possessed; and the story ends, 'And everyone was amazed'. We will be quiet for a moment, to allow ourselves to be amazed again at all that Jesus has done for us.

Prayers of the Faithful
Jesus heals this man and then sends him to tell people what the Lord has done for him. We think of all that Jesus has done for us, all our healing. We offer ourselves to be a gift and inspiration to others around us.

We think of people who, like the man in this gospel, suffer terrible anguish and are out of control of their lives. We think of families and friends who try to care for them.

WEEK FOUR – TUESDAY

Mark 5:21–43 (Jairus' daughter)

Introduction to Mass
In today's gospel we see people sick and suffering, and family members desperately worried. Let us start our prayer by bringing before the Lord all the suffering and worry we are aware of, in ourselves and in others around us.

Prayers of the Faithful
The story of Jairus' daughter invites us to think of children who are sick, and their families who care and worry. May they feel Christ's healing touch.

We hear of a woman who had suffered from a haemorrhage for twelve years. We pray for people who have been suffering for long years. We ask for courage to reach out and touch the Lord.

ORDINARY TIME

WEEK FOUR – WEDNESDAY

Mark 6:1–6 (he was amazed at their lack of faith)

Introduction to Mass
When Jesus comes to his home town, he is 'amazed at their lack of faith'. We come before him now, humbly, with our little faith, and ask for his mercy and strength.

Prayers of the Faithful
The people could not believe that one of their own was God's special prophet. We think of ordinary people around us who are 'prophets', who show God to us. May we allow ourselves to be inspired by them.

Could Jesus be saying to us what he said to them, that he was amazed at their lack of faith? We pray for all churchgoers. May we not presume our faith is perfect. May we open ourselves to deeper faith.

WEEK FOUR – THURSDAY

Mark 6:7–13 (the twelve sent out in pairs)

Introduction to Mass
Welcome is a theme in our gospel today, so we begin by quietly reflecting on welcome. God's welcoming arms embrace each of us here. And in our hearts we say 'welcome' to the Lord and 'welcome' to one another.

Prayers of the Faithful
As Jesus sent out the apostles in pairs, so we pray for a spirit of partnership in our Christian community. May we work together with humility and mutual appreciation, encouraging one another.

We pray for a spirit of welcome and hospitality in our community. We pray for all who are trying to reach out to others with a message of friendship and community.

WEEK FOUR – FRIDAY

Mark 6:14–29 (beheading of John the Baptist)

Introduction to Mass
We come together, as we do at every Eucharist, to give thanks. We begin with a quiet pause. What do I want to give thanks for today?

Prayers of the Faithful
The death of John the Baptist prefigures the death of Jesus. We give thanks to God for all who have died in the name of Christ, all the martyrs, all who died innocently while serving him. May God hold them close to His heart.

The death of John the Baptist reminds us of how much senseless death and suffering are caused by the greed and the whims of others. May the world learn to put respect for others before personal self-interest.

WEEK FOUR – SATURDAY

Mark 6:30–34 ('rest for a while')

Introduction to Mass
'You must come away', Jesus says, 'and rest a while'. Let us take up his invitation. May our time at Mass today be special time where we rest with him and find peace.

Prayers of the Faithful
Jesus takes his companions away from the bustle and pressure to rest. May we allow Jesus to take us too, to take us away for a while from the demands of our lives, to spend time resting with him.

Jesus took pity on the crowd, 'like sheep without a shepherd'. We think of people who are lost or searching. We pray that our leaders will be compassionate guides.

WEEK FIVE – MONDAY

Mark 6:53–56 (all who touched him were cured)

Introduction to Mass
In today's gospel scene, all who touched Jesus were cured. In a quiet moment now, we reach out to touch Jesus with our faith – we want his life to flow through us.

Prayers of the Faithful
We thank God for the gift of touch. May we use this gift to touch others with our friendship and our care, and to bring hope and joy. May we allow others to touch us too with their love and support.

The people in today's gospel were thinking, not of themselves, but of the sick, and of bringing them to Jesus. May our community be filled with the same thoughtfulness, the same desire to be of help to others.

WEEK FIVE – TUESDAY

Mark 7:1–13 (God's word and human traditions)

Introduction to Mass
There's a phrase about prayer that is echoed in today's gospel: 'better a heart without words than words without heart'. So we begin, without words, in silence, opening our hearts to God.

Prayers of the Faithful
May our following of Christ be more than just lip-service. May it always be heartfelt, and from the heart, and full of heart. May our serving God come from the depths of our hearts.

Jesus talks about putting religious traditions before God's commandments. We pray for our Church. May it not cling to anything other than God. May it have a spirit of openness, willing to hear God's word in new ways.

WEEK FIVE – WEDNESDAY

Mark 7:14–23 (what comes from the heart)

Introduction to Mass
Jesus says to the people: 'listen to me and understand'. We pause now. We leave aside our thoughts and preoccupations; we prepare ourselves to listen to Jesus speaking to us.

Prayers of the Faithful
For Jesus, the heart is what matters. We pray for integrity of heart. We pray for a pure heart. May God help make our intentions pure, uncorrupted by evil.

We pray for all whose hearts are confused, torn or divided. We pray for all who are trying to understand their own hearts. May all God's people find their true selves.

WEEK FIVE – THURSDAY

Mark 7:24–30 (the Syro–Phoenician woman)

Introduction to Mass
We begin with a quiet moment. Like the woman in today's gospel, we approach Jesus in our need, with courage and determination and faith.

Prayers of the Faithful
This gospel tells us that there is no limit to God's outreach; it embraces all. So we pray for people of different faiths and convictions. We give thanks for the faith and belief that people have.

In the spirit of today's gospel, we pray for people who are caring for a son or daughter who is ill. In their worry and anxiety, may they find God's presence and strength and support.

WEEK FIVE – FRIDAY

Mark 7:31–37 ('ephphatha' – 'be opened')

Introduction to Mass
In today's Mass, Jesus takes aside a man who is deaf and has a speech impediment. He puts his fingers into his ears and touches his mouth with spittle, and says, 'be opened'. For a moment now, we let Jesus take us aside and touch us and heal us.

Prayers of the Faithful
We pray for all whose hearing is impaired and all who suffer a speech impediment. May they have courage in their hearts. May they enrich the lives of those around them.

This gospel is the source of a prayer in our Baptism ceremony, where the priest touches the ears and mouth of the one to be baptised. I now say that prayer for all of us here: 'May the Lord touch your ears to receive his word and your mouth to proclaim his faith, to the praise and glory of God the Father.'

WEEK FIVE – SATURDAY

Mark 8:1–10 (feeding of the four thousand)

Introduction to Mass
Today's gospel story, where Jesus feeds four thousand in the desert, prefigures our own Eucharist. Let us each for a moment think of our own 'desert' – our hunger, our barrenness, our poverty, our desolation. Let us wait on Jesus to look on us with compassion.

Prayers of the Faithful
The gospel makes us mindful of the hunger in our world. We know that there is enough for all – and so we ask the Lord to teach all people the miracle of sharing.

We pray for people who cannot feed themselves. We thank God for the friends who come to their help. May we learn from them to accept help with dignity and grace.

WEEK SIX – MONDAY

Mark 8:11–13 ('no sign shall be given')

Introduction to Mass
Part of the message in today's gospel is that, in Jesus, God has given us all we could need or want. Let us pause in grateful silence, with thankful hearts – in Jesus, God has given us all we could need or want.

Prayers of the Faithful
People can be very demanding, always looking for more and more. May we learn to appreciate what we have, and simply to enjoy what we are already blessed with in Christ.

The gospel talks of 'signs'. In the 1960s, the Vatican Council coined the phrase, 'reading the signs of the times'. May we Christians learn to do this, to be open and attentive to what the Spirit is saying to us in events around us.

WEEK SIX – TUESDAY

Mark 8:14–21 ('do you not yet understand?')

Introduction to Mass
We are encouraged by Jesus in today's Word to remember – he is the one bread, we are one body in him. Our quiet prayer as we begin is to dwell for a moment on our unity in him – our togetherness, our solidarity.

Prayers of the Faithful
Jesus asks his disciples a series of seven questions. Imagine him asking us – Do you not understand? Are your minds closed? Have you no perception? Do you not remember? May the Spirit of Jesus open our hearts, to help us see and understand.

The number of baskets is symbolic in this gospel. 'Twelve' stands for the Jewish world, 'seven' for the Gentile world. Both are brought together in Jesus. May the world come to see that all of us – all peoples and all religions – are one in God's loving embrace.

WEEK SIX – WEDNESDAY

Mark 8:22–26 (blind man)

Introduction to Mass
In today's gospel Jesus touches a blind man and he begins to see again. We pause to reflect for a moment. We are all spiritually blind in some way. We ask Jesus to help us to see.

Prayers of the Faithful
The blind man is cured gradually. It is a symbol of our Christian life – a gradual enlightenment and coming to see. We ask God to protect us from being self-satisfied or self-righteous. May we always be willing to see anew, always open to being enlightened.

Many among us have the opposite experience to the man in the gospel. We think of all who are gradually losing their sight. May they not become depressed. May they have courage to adapt with hopeful hearts.

WEEK SIX – THURSDAY

Mark 8:27–33 ('you are the Christ')

Introduction to Mass
We begin with a moment of silent adoration. We think of Peter's profession of faith in today's gospel. With Peter we say to Jesus, 'You are the Christ'.

Prayers of the Faithful
We pray for all Christians, that our eyes will be opened, to see more clearly the true face of Christ, in whom God's own heart is revealed to us.

The disciples find it hard to see that Jesus must walk the path of suffering. May we be willing to accept the suffering involved in following him. May we be willing to pay the price to make our dreams come true.

WEEK SIX – FRIDAY

Mark 8:34–9:1 ('take up your cross')

Introduction to Mass
What we all share in common is that we are following Christ – the theme of today's gospel. Let us pause for a moment to think of how much he means to us.

Prayers of the Faithful
We pray for courage – not to be embarrassed or ashamed about our faith – courage to renounce ourselves and to find our true selves in Christ.

We thank God for the people who have inspired us in our following Christ, through their courage and commitment and hope. We think of them and ask God to bless them.

WEEK SIX – SATURDAY

Mark 9:2–13 (transfiguration)

Introduction to Mass
In the gospel today, Jesus takes Peter and James and John up a mountain so that they can be alone by themselves. Now, in this Eucharist, Jesus invites us to come away with him for a while. In quiet prayer, we enter into his presence.

Prayers of the Faithful
The transfiguration was a major moment of revelation for Peter and James and John. Let us thank God for such moments in our own lives – special times when God has come close to us, when our love for God has been deepened.

The Father says, 'This is my son, the beloved'. God the Father says similar words to each of us. 'You are my beloved'. May each one know in their heart that they are God's beloved.

ORDINARY TIME

WEEK SEVEN – MONDAY

Mark 9:14–29 (help my unbelief)

Introduction to Mass
The father in today's gospel cries out to Jesus: 'I do have faith; help the little faith I have'. We make this our own sentiment as we approach the Lord, aware of our need to entrust ourselves completely to him.

Prayers of the Faithful
In this gospel, the disciples are powerless without Jesus. So we pray that our own trust in him will be boundless. May we set no limits to what God's power can achieve in us and through us.

Thinking of the father and son, we pray for parents who look after a suffering son or daughter, year after year. We praise God for their love. May they always know God's power in the pain of their lives.

WEEK SEVEN – TUESDAY

Mark 9:30–37 (last of all and servant of all)

Introduction to Mass
In today's gospel, Jesus is instructing his disciples. In quiet prayer we now ask him to instruct us – to teach us through the Word we listen to – to open our eyes to recognise him in the breaking of bread.

Prayers of the Faithful
Jesus teaches us the spirit of true disciples. As we follow him to the cross, may we choose humility and not status; service instead of power; gentleness in place of force.

Jesus set a child before them. We thank God for our children and we pray that they will teach us to be open and receptive, to be grateful and life-giving.

WEEK SEVEN – WEDNESDAY

Mark 9:38–40 (anyone not against us is for us)

Introduction to Mass
In the spirit of today's gospel, we begin Mass with a prayer of thanks in our hearts – thanks for the people who are good to us – and thanks for the good we do for others.

Prayers of the Faithful
'Anyone who is not against us is for us.' Jesus teaches us to be appreciative of wherever and whenever people are doing good – including when they are not 'one of us'. May we be generous in our appreciation of people.

We thank God for all the ways in which the Spirit is at work – in people who bring hope – in people who are a light in the world.

WEEK SEVEN – THURSDAY

Mark 9:41–50 (if your hand should cause you to sin)

Introduction to Mass
Jesus asks us, in today's gospel, to examine ourselves, to ask: is there anything in us that is causing us to sin? So, quietly, we ask ourselves that question – knowing how much he believes in us.

Prayers of the Faithful
'To bring down one of these little ones who have faith' – possibly the worst sin of all for Jesus, to scandalise, upset or discourage the humble, the 'little ones' among us. That we may all heed his teaching, we pray.

Jesus tells us: 'Have salt in yourselves'. May his Spirit bring new life and vitality to our faith, and save us from deadness and routine. May the fire of discipleship burn strong in our hearts.

ORDINARY TIME

WEEK SEVEN – FRIDAY

Mark 10:1–12 (divorce)

Introduction to Mass
Today, Jesus teaches about marriage and divorce. So let us begin by bringing into our prayers and our Mass our friends and neighbours who are married, as well as those we know who are separated or struggling. We pause a moment to think of them.

Prayers of the Faithful
Jesus presents us with the ideal for marriage. We pray for our families. May God keep us faithful to each other, and increase our feeling of belonging.

We pray for those whose relationship has failed. In disappointment or guilt, betrayal or failure, may God's undying love give them future and give them hope.

WEEK SEVEN – SATURDAY

Mark 10:13–16 ('let the little children come to me')

Introduction to Mass
Jesus says: 'Let the little children come to me'. We pause for a moment, as God's children, to come to him, to rest in his embrace – with the simple trust of a child, with the assurance of a child, with the joy of a child.

Prayers of the Faithful
Jesus invites us to welcome the kingdom of God like a little child. May we all rediscover the joy and the newness of the gospel. May we discover our sheer appreciation for what we believe.

We pray for the children in our community. May they know how much Jesus loves them. May they grow up safe and be happy. And we thank God for how they enrich our lives.

WEEK EIGHT – MONDAY

Mark 10:17–27 (the rich man)

Introduction to Mass
In our gospel, a rich man asks Jesus: 'What must I do to inherit eternal life?' Let us ask the same question. Quietly for a moment, we ask Jesus to show us what we must do to enter more fully into his life.

Prayers of the Faithful
It has been called the saddest story in the gospel, the only one where somebody refused to follow Jesus. We pray for anybody who is struggling to let go and to give themselves. May they know that Jesus loves them.

We pray for wealthy people. May all of us, rich or poor, have the wisdom to know what really matters. May all of us be free from enslavement to possessions. Whatever our circumstances, may we be true to Christ and true to ourselves.

WEEK EIGHT – TUESDAY

Mark 10:28–31 ('what about us?')

Introduction to Mass
Peter says to Jesus, 'we have left everything and followed you'. We pause a moment to reflect on how much Jesus means to us, the place he has taken up in our hearts, how committed we have become.

Prayers of the Faithful
The gospel talks about leaving everything. We ask God to bless women and men in religious life. May they inspire all of us to give ourselves to Christ each day of our lives, in everything we do.

The gospel talks about persecution. We think of fellow Christians in different parts of the world who are suffering discrimination, injustice and persecution. We reach out to them with our prayer.

WEEK EIGHT – WEDNESDAY

Mark 10:32–45 (the Son of Man came to serve)

Introduction to Mass
Jesus asks James and John: what do you want me to do for you? It turns out that they do not know what they are asking. We can apply this to ourselves too. Let us quietly call on Jesus to guide us to our true desires and needs.

Prayers of the Faithful
'This is not to happen among you.' We pray that our Church will be freed from the temptations of power and from authoritarianism. May leadership be exercised in Jesus' spirit of service.

James and John are gripped by selfish ambition. We pray that our own discipleship will be pure. May we be willing to follow Jesus in the path of generous self-giving.

WEEK EIGHT – THURSDAY

Mark 10:46–52 (Bartimaeus)

Introduction to Mass
In today's gospel, Bartimaeus cries out to Jesus: 'Son of David, have pity on me'. We make the same prayer. In our need, we silently ask Jesus to show us his compassion.

Prayers of the Faithful
Jesus asks Bartimaeus the same question he asked James and John in yesterday's gospel: what do you want me to do for you? But Bartimaeus, although blind, could see. He could see who Jesus was, and was in touch with his own needs. May all of us, blind or sighted, be blessed with inner vision and understanding.

We pray for people who are blind, or whose vision is impaired or failing. We ask God to bless those who work with and for blind people. May all have courage and encouragement.

WEEK EIGHT – FRIDAY

Mark 11:11–26 (Jesus clears the temple)

Introduction to Mass
Jesus says to us today: when you stand in prayer, forgive whatever you have against anybody, so that God may forgive your failings too. In the quiet of our hearts, we ask for a forgiving heart.

Prayers of the Faithful
The withered fig tree symbolises the end of the temple. For Jesus has replaced the temple. He is the new temple where God is to be found. May we place all our faith in him.

'My house will be called a house of prayer.' We thank God for this place of prayer where we come to worship. May many others feel its welcome, and come to find the presence and peace of God here.

WEEK EIGHT – SATURDAY

Mark 11:27–33 (Jesus' authority)

Introduction to Mass
Eucharist means thanksgiving, and we gather to give thanks to God for Jesus. Let us now, in the quiet of our hearts, bring to the Lord all that we are thankful for in our lives.

Prayers of the Faithful
The priests and scribes and elders sit on the fence. We, however, are gathered here because of our shared conviction that Jesus' authority comes from God. May we entrust ourselves completely to him.

We pray for people who are searching for truth and for light – for something they can place their trust in and give their hearts to. May God's Spirit guide them in their quest.

WEEK NINE – MONDAY

Mark 12:1–12 (he sent his beloved son)

Introduction to Mass
Today's gospel is about accepting Jesus as God's beloved Son. We gather here because we have accepted him. Now we open our hearts to welcome and accept him more deeply than before.

Prayers of the Faithful
The gospel shows the leaders of God's people rejecting the prophets and then rejecting Jesus. We pray that the leaders in our Christian community will recognise and listen to the prophetic voices in our Church and in our world.

The vineyard is given to others. The gospel is also saying that the good news is for all people. We pray for all God's people, of different convictions and different religions. May the spark of divine life be alive in all.

WEEK NINE – TUESDAY

Mark 12:13–17 (give to Caesar what belongs to Caesar)

Introduction to Mass
There's a remark in today's gospel that, for Jesus, a person's rank meant nothing. So we know that we all come before Jesus absolutely equal in dignity, equally beloved. Quietly we take this into our hearts.

Prayers of the Faithful
We see people whose relating to Jesus is full of hypocrisy. We pray that our own relationship to Jesus will be honest and openhearted.

Caesar and God. We pray for all Christians as they seek to balance their commitment to God with their commitment to the State. We pray for courage and honesty, especially in difficult issues.

WEEK NINE – WEDNESDAY

Mark 12:18–27 (God is God of the living)

Introduction to Mass
Today's gospel invites us to believe in the life-giving power of God. So now, for a quiet moment, whatever our situation, whatever our need, we open ourselves to God's power to breathe new life in us.

Prayers of the Faithful
'He is God of the living.' And so we think of our beloved who have died – encouraged by Jesus' picture of who God is – a God who transforms those who die into new existence.

We pray that resurrection will be our mindset. May we open ourselves to new life. May we believe in the capacity to be transformed. May we always look out for the signs of hope in our midst.

WEEK NINE – THURSDAY

Mark 12:28–34 (love God, love your neighbour)

Introduction to Mass
Today Jesus gives us his great teaching – to love God and love our neighbour. But first, let us think for a moment of God, the source of all love – God, whose love makes us lovable and able to love.

Prayers of the Faithful
May we love God with our whole selves – in wonder and gratitude and closeness. May God be the love of our lives. May all God's people find God in their lives.

May we love others as we would like to be loved ourselves – with real respect, with appreciation for their grace and beauty. May all God's people experience love in their lives.

WEEK NINE – FRIDAY

Mark 12:35–37 (Christ is the Son of David)

Introduction to Mass
Our gospel points us to Jesus the Son of God, seated at the right hand of the Father. We begin our Mass by entering into his welcoming presence, hearts filled with faith and trust.

Prayers of the Faithful
'The people heard this with delight.' May our experience of the gospel be one of delight. May Jesus delight our hearts with the knowledge of God's love. May Christian living be a delightful thing for us.

'I will put your enemies under your feet.' We ask for the Lord's power, to help conquer the enemies inside us – temptations, compulsions, or whatever is blocking up the love within us.

WEEK NINE – SATURDAY

Mark 12:38–44 (the poor widow)

Introduction to Mass
Jesus teaches us today that the most important gift we can make is to give ourselves. Let us think quietly for a moment – of the gift that each one of us is, of the gift that each of us can be.

Prayers of the Faithful
We pray for people who feel that they have little to give. May they come to see how rich they are. May we all find joy in giving ourselves and giving our time.

We pray for those among us who are widowed. May they go on hearing the call to love. May they continue to enrich others with their love.

WEEK TEN – MONDAY

Matthew 5:1–12 (beatitudes)

Introduction to Mass
Today's gospel is the Beatitudes – and it invites us to rejoice. Not because we're fortunate, because many are not. But we can rejoice even in our troubles. We rejoice because God sees us. We pause a moment.

Prayers of the Faithful
In our gospel Jesus talks about the 'little people' of the world. We thank God for the gift they are to all of us – those who trust in God, the gentle, those mourning, the merciful, the pure in heart, the peacemakers, those who hunger for what is right and just.

We pray for ourselves – that we will trust and serve God, that we will radiate a gentle, peace-filled disposition, that we will be filled with compassion and strive for what is right and just.

WEEK TEN – TUESDAY

Matthew 5:13–16 (salt, light)

Introduction to Mass
To begin our Mass, we rest with Jesus' words to his disciples: You are the salt of the earth; You are the light of the world. We become aware of our calling. We accept into our hearts that we are, each of us, a gift, with something to offer in the world.

Prayers of the Faithful
We are 'salt'. We ask that God's Spirit renew our enthusiasm, to inspire us with a new sense of our calling, encourage us to believe in what we have to offer.

We are 'light'. May our Christian community be a light in this corner of the world. May we work together to make Christ more visible.

WEEK TEN – WEDNESDAY

Matthew 5:17–19 (not to abolish, but to complete)

Introduction to Mass
Jesus is presented to us in today's gospel as the fulfilment of everything that has gone before. We stay with this thought for a moment. He is our fulfilment, our everything, our point of reference, our beginning and our end.

Prayers of the Faithful
Jesus teaches the importance of the law of Moses. We pray that we will be people of principle and integrity. We praise all those in our society who are a witness through their commitment to moral values.

Jesus is the fulfilment of the law. May our faith in him and our commitment to him inspire us to live authentic lives, witnessing to true moral values.

WEEK TEN – THURSDAY

Matthew 5:20–26 (be reconciled)

Introduction to Mass
Jesus tells us today to be reconciled before we come to the altar. So, in our hearts, let us pray for anybody we have differences or difficulties with. Let us wish them peace.

Prayers of the Faithful
We pray that none of us will do anything to add to the violence in the world, through our thoughts or through our reactions. May we not be controlled by our anger but, rather, by our love.

We think of people who are victims of violence – in a relationship or in their family or in their community. We reach out to them in their fear. We touch them with our prayer.

WEEK TEN – FRIDAY

Matthew 5:27–32 (adultery, divorce)

Introduction to Mass
Jesus teaches in our gospel about faithfulness in marriage. So we begin by thinking about faithfulness – especially, God's faithful, unequivocal, irreversible love for us. We pause a moment with grateful hearts.

Prayers of the Faithful
Jesus talks about adultery. We think of people who are married and how seriously they take being faithful. We pray that their love will always protect them. We pray for any who are tempted to be unfaithful.

Jesus talks about divorce. We pray for people whose marriage has broken down, especially for those who have been betrayed. We ask God's life-giving hope for them.

WEEK TEN – SATURDAY

Matthew 5:33–37 (do not swear)

Introduction to Mass
We begin our prayer, in the spirit of today's gospel, by bringing to mind how God has said a resounding 'Yes' to each one of us in Christ. In the quiet of our hearts, we say 'Yes' to God in response.

Prayers of the Faithful
Jesus teaches us to be so honest and reliable, that we will have no need to swear oaths at all. May the words we speak to each other be honest. May others find us faithful and reliable and kind.

We pray for a world where truth and truthfulness can be in short supply. We thank God for courageous people, who seek to uncover the truth where there are lies and deception.

WEEK ELEVEN – MONDAY

Matthew 5:38–42 (the other cheek)

Introduction to Mass
Each day these weeks we are listening to the Sermon on the Mount – Jesus challenging us to challenge ourselves, to go further in our Christian living. We ask him now to forgive us our complacency and to give us a share of his Spirit.

Prayers of the Faithful
We pray that we will react well when we are treated badly. May we learn not to retaliate, but to conquer evil with good. May we surprise others with our love.

May all Christians be generous in their response to others. May all be inspired by Jesus to go the extra mile; to do more rather than less; to give more rather than less.

WEEK ELEVEN – TUESDAY

Matthew 5:43–48 (love your enemies)

Introduction to Mass
Jesus encourages us today to love our enemies. So let us think for a moment of anybody we are estranged from. And let us think of God, who loves each one of us with the same passion.

Prayers of the Faithful
We all need divine help when it comes to loving our enemies. We pray that we will be able to think kindly of them. May we see a halo over their heads and bless them.

We think of the many situations in our world where people are divided by hatred. We pray that people will see God's image in one another. We pray for the transforming power of non-violent love.

WEEK ELEVEN – WEDNESDAY

Matthew 6:1–6, 16–18 (prayer, fasting, almsgiving)

Introduction to Mass
In today's gospel, Jesus speaks to us three times of 'your Father, who sees all that is done in secret'. Let us now, for a moment, enter into the inner chamber of our heart, that secret place within, where God dwells.

Prayers of the Faithful
We pray for a pure heart. May our motives go beyond the desire for approval and admiration. May we do what is right and good for its own sake – because it is right and good.

We pray for young people, growing up into adulthood. May they be drawn to true values. May they see beyond what is superficial or selfish, to what really matters.

WEEK ELEVEN – THURSDAY

Matthew 6:7–15 (our Father)

Introduction to Mass
In giving us the *Our Father*, Jesus says, 'your Father knows what you need before you ask'. So we leave our words aside for a moment, to be quiet with the Lord, who already knows what we need.

Prayers of the Faithful
In the spirit of Jesus' prayer, we focus ourselves on God. We pray that God's kingdom will have a central place in our hearts. We commit ourselves to the coming about of God's kingdom among God's people.

In the spirit of Jesus' prayer, we confidently ask God's help. May God nourish and sustain us. May God give us the spirit of forgiveness. May God protect us from evil.

WEEK ELEVEN – FRIDAY

Matthew 6:19–23 (where your treasure is)

Introduction to Mass
'Where your treasure is, there will your heart be also.' For a quiet moment, we consider these words of Jesus. He is our treasure. Our hearts belong with him.

Prayers of the Faithful
May each of us, in our hearts, always be attracted to what is truly to be treasured. May we spend the love in our hearts on what truly matters – on one another, on God, on those who are suffering.

The eye is the lamp of the body. When we look around us, may we look with eyes of compassion, with eyes of hope. May our eyes be filled with the light of love.

WEEK ELEVEN – SATURDAY

Matthew 6:24–34 (set your hearts on God's kingdom)

Introduction to Mass
The theme of today's gospel is trusting in God. So, for a moment, we quietly rest ourselves in God – like a child in its mother's arms, in trust and peace.

Prayers of the Faithful
'Set your hearts on God's kingdom first.' We all have material, practical concerns in our lives. But we pray not to be consumed by them. May trust in God protect us from overwhelming anxiety.

We pray for all among us who lack enough to eat or enough to wear – all who lack the necessities of life. May we, by our practical support, ease the worry in their lives.

WEEK TWELVE – MONDAY

Matthew 7:1–5 (do not judge)

Introduction to Mass
In the Sermon on the Mount, Jesus tells us not to judge. Let us begin our prayer by remembering God – who does not condemn us, but understands us and sees what is best in us.

Prayers of the Faithful
It's often easier to criticise others than to criticise ourselves. We pray that we may humbly acknowledge our own shortcomings. May this help us to be generous in our view of others.

We pray for our Church, that people will find it to be a place of acceptance, and not judgment. May we, as a community, communicate to others the welcoming face of God.

WEEK TWELVE – TUESDAY

Matthew 7:6, 12–14 (treat others as you would like to be treated)

Introduction to Mass
We begin, in the spirit of today's gospel, by reflecting quietly on how God treats each one of us – how generously, how graciously. How blessed we are to know God's infinite compassion and understanding.

Prayers of the Faithful
'Treat others as you would like them to treat you.' May we treat each other in the same way that God treats us. May all our relationships be characterised by grace and generosity, understanding and compassion.

'Enter by the narrow gate.' The path to life is free; and yet it demands something of us. May we be willing to pay the price to make our dreams come true.

ORDINARY TIME

WEEK TWELVE – WEDNESDAY

Matthew 7:15–20 (by their fruits)

Introduction to Mass
Today's gospel is about putting faith into action. To do that, we rely on God's strength and inspiration. So now, in silence, we open our hearts to divine power and divine energy.

Prayers of the Faithful
'A sound tree produces good fruit.' May our faith be visible in our actions. Each day may we look for ways of translating our faith into action.

'You can tell them by their fruits.' We thank God for the people who inspire us – people who live their faith, people who live for the truth and for true values.

WEEK TWELVE – THURSDAY

Matthew 7:21–29 (house built on rock)

Introduction to Mass
The Word of the Lord is the rock we build our lives on. As we enter into this Mass, in our hearts we ask the Lord to give us ears to hear his word, and courage to take up its challenge.

Prayers of the Faithful
'It is not those who say Lord, Lord.' May God preserve us from thinking that piety and prayer and devotion is enough. May we act on his word, put it into action, and do his will.

Thinking of the image in the gospel, we pray for people who have lost their homes or are homeless. And we pray for victims of landslides, earthquakes, flooding and storms.

WEEK TWELVE – FRIDAY

Matthew 8:1–4 (Jesus heals a leper)

Introduction to Mass
In our gospel, a leper comes and bows low before Jesus, saying: 'if you want, you can cure me'. We now come before Jesus. We bow our hearts low in reverence. And we ask him to heal us.

Prayers of the Faithful
Jesus says to the leper: 'of course I want to cure you'. May we take into our hearts how much Jesus wants to do for us. May we open ourselves to his healing power.

Thinking of the leper, we pray for all who suffer from skin diseases or from disfigurement of their body. May they, and we, never lose sight of their grace and beauty.

WEEK TWELVE – SATURDAY

Matthew 8:5–17 (the centurion)

Introduction to Mass
Today's gospel gives us the prayer: 'Lord I am not worthy to receive you; only say the word and I will be healed'. We now say the prayer in our hearts. We come before the Lord, unworthy, but filled with faith.

Prayers of the Faithful
'Nowhere in Israel have I found faith like this.' Let us give thanks for faith, for all the ways faith in God manifests itself in the world – in the Church and outside, among Christians and among other religions and beliefs.

This gospel is full of healing. So we think now of all among us who are sick or paralysed or possessed by evil forces. And we ask Jesus for a share in his compassion.

WEEK THIRTEEN – MONDAY

Matthew 8:18–22 (follow me)

Introduction to Mass
Jesus says to us today: 'follow me'. This is what unites us here. We are all his followers. In a spirit of community and solidarity, let us now pray quietly for one another, companions on the journey.

Prayers of the Faithful
'Follow me.' We all need to hear Jesus' call as if for the first time. May we give his call priority in our lives. Each day may we discover new meaning in his call.

We pray for all among us who find it difficult to follow Jesus. We ask God's Spirit to enlighten and reassure and comfort and encourage all who are drawn to him.

WEEK THIRTEEN – TUESDAY

Matthew 8:23–27 (storm on the lake)

Introduction to Mass
In our gospel, Jesus calms the storm. All of us have stormy or turbulent times in our lives. Now we turn to Jesus, in a moment of quiet, to feel his calming presence in our hearts.

Prayers of the Faithful
'Save us, Lord, we are going down!' We pray for people whose lives are in turmoil, whose peace has been shattered, who feel desperate. We reach out to them with love in our hearts.

'Why so frightened, you of little faith?' We pray for ourselves. When we are afraid, may our faith grow, to conquer our fear. May we entrust ourselves to the Lord of our lives.

WEEK THIRTEEN – WEDNESDAY

Matthew 8:28–34 (two demoniacs)

Introduction to Mass
Our gospel today shows the power of Jesus to change people's lives. All of us want to be changed by him for the better. For a moment in silence, let us open ourselves to his power.

Prayers of the Faithful
An extraordinary story – but at the heart of it are two lives transformed by Jesus. We pray for all who yearn to be transformed. And may we ourselves believe in our capacity to be transformed by the Lord.

The whole town implores Jesus to leave. He can have an upsetting effect in people's lives. May all his followers come to understand him more. May all be open to learning new things from him.

WEEK THIRTEEN – THURSDAY

Matthew 9:1–8 (paralysed man)

Introduction to Mass
People bring a paralysed man to Jesus in our gospel. In the same spirit, let us begin by bringing to Jesus people we know who are sick or infirm or suffering. We pause to think of them and make them part of our Mass.

Prayers of the Faithful
'They praised God for giving such power to human beings.' We too praise God for such forgiving love. We pray that we all discover within ourselves the power to forgive, the power of forgiving.

People carry the paralysed man to Jesus. We think of people to are carrying somebody else, minding someone who is dependent or carrying someone's burden with them.

ORDINARY TIME

WEEK THIRTEEN – FRIDAY

Matthew 9:9–13 (eating with sinners)

Introduction to Mass
Let us begin by listening quietly in our hearts as Jesus speaks to us the words he speaks to Matthew in today's gospel. In our hearts, we hear him saying to each of us: 'Follow me'.

Prayers of the Faithful
Today we see what was closest to Jesus' heart – that is, bringing God's welcoming embrace to all who found themselves out in the cold. May we be a welcoming, inclusive community in his name.

'What I want is mercy, not sacrifice.' For Jesus, compassion was everything. May our own prayer and devotion always lead us out of ourselves and into the practice of compassionate love.

WEEK THIRTEEN – SATURDAY

Matthew 9:14–17 (new wineskins)

Introduction to Mass
Jesus is about something new happening in our lives – the theme of today's gospel. So we open our hearts to 'newness'. We pray in our hearts for God's Spirit to come to us in new ways, to open new paths to us.

Prayers of the Faithful
New wineskins and old – both are preserved. May our lives achieve a balance of new and old. May we cherish what has stood us well in our faith. May we embrace new ways and explore new paths.

We pray for our Church. As it holds on faithfully to traditions from past generations, may it engage with today's world in a spirit of exploration, to discover new graces.

WEEK FOURTEEN – MONDAY

Matthew 9:18–26 (two healings)

Introduction to Mass
Again in today's gospel, we witness Jesus' healing powers. But we also see the faith that two people have in his power. We now, in silent prayer, put our faith in Jesus' power to heal us and make us whole.

Prayers of the Faithful
We think of the little girl in the story. And we pray for all girls and boys with life-threatening conditions or serious suffering. And we pray for their parents and families.

We think of the woman suffering for twelve years. And we pray for all whose suffering has been long-lasting. May they not lose heart or hope. May they be a gift to us all.

WEEK FOURTEEN – TUESDAY

Matthew 9:32–38 (Jesus proclaims the good news)

Introduction to Mass
In word and action, Jesus proclaims the good news of God's kingdom. We gather here to proclaim him as our Lord. We rejoice in the good news of God's love for us in Jesus. We rest our hearts in his compassion.

Prayers of the Faithful
Jesus felt compassion for the crowds, harassed and dejected. We pray for all among us who are harassed or dejected. We ask the Lord to lift the spirits of all who are trying to cope with the pressures of life.

'Send labourers to the harvest.' May we each hear the call of Jesus, and respond. May we reach out to others in the spirit of Jesus, inspired with his compassion.

WEEK FOURTEEN – WEDNESDAY

Matthew 10:1–7 (Jesus calls the twelve)

Introduction to Mass
One by one, in today's gospel, we hear the names of the twelve apostles, as Jesus calls them. In the quiet of our hearts, let us listen to his voice saying our name, as he calls each one of us by name.

Prayers of the Faithful
The 'disciples' are here called 'apostles' because they are being sent. We too are sent, to be Christ's body and to do Christ's work. May we be aware of being sent, each day of our lives.

'The kingdom of heaven is close at hand.' God's grace is close at hand, but we do not often realise it. Lord, bless us with the gift of stillness. Help us be aware of your nearness at all times.

WEEK FOURTEEN – THURSDAY

Matthew 10:7–15 (Jesus sends the twelve)

Introduction to Mass
In the spirit of today's gospel, we begin Mass by opening the doors of our hearts to welcome Jesus, to listen to what he has to say and to let his peace descend upon us.

Prayers of the Faithful
'You received without charge, give without charge.' We give thanks for the free gift of God's undying love. May we live our lives in the same spirit of generous giving.

The twelve go from house to house. We pray for all in our parishes who are involved in the ministry of visiting people's homes. May people find in them the welcoming, listening, caring face of the Christian community.

WEEK FOURTEEN – FRIDAY

Matthew 10:16–23 (the Spirit will be speaking in you)

Introduction to Mass
The word 'Mass' comes from the word for sending, or mission. In today's gospel, Jesus continues to instruct the twelve as he sends them out. May he guide and strengthen us during this Mass, for we too are sent.

Prayers of the Faithful
Jesus warns of the adversity and suffering involved in proclaiming the gospel. We thank God for all who have suffered, and all who now suffer, for the sake of the gospel. May their witness inspire us.

'Do not worry what to say, the Spirit will be speaking in you.' May each of us carry Jesus in our hearts. May his Spirit grow within us, day by day, and inspire in us the right words and responses, wherever we go.

WEEK FOURTEEN – SATURDAY

Matthew 10:24–33 (do not be afraid)

Introduction to Mass
Three times in our gospel Jesus says to the twelve, 'Do not be afraid'. Let us be quiet for a moment, as he speaks the same words to us, his disciples: 'Do not be afraid'.

Prayers of the Faithful
'Do not be afraid.' We pray especially for the leaders in our Church and in our Christian community. In difficult times, may our leaders be blessed with the assurance of God's Spirit. May they grow in courage.

'Do not be afraid.' We ask the Lord to breathe his gentle spirit on all who are gripped by fear – fear of the future, fear of another person, fear of the unknown, fear of letting go or some other fear.

WEEK FIFTEEN – MONDAY

Matthew 10:34–11:1 (not peace, but a sword)

Introduction to Mass
We listen to Jesus' words today: 'those who welcome me welcome the one who sent me'. We pause for a moment to welcome Jesus into our midst, for in welcoming him, we welcome our God.

Prayers of the Faithful
Jesus' words sound harsh, divisive. But it's to make a point – that following him is decisive. May we be single-minded as his disciples, holding back nothing, as we seek him in all things.

We pray for a welcoming heart. May we welcome the truth, whoever it is that points us to it. May we welcome all God's messengers – the prophets, the holy people – who come our way, whoever they may be.

WEEK FIFTEEN – TUESDAY

Matthew 11:20–24 (they refused to repent)

Introduction to Mass
In our gospel, Jesus reproaches those who refuse to repent. Now, in the silence of our hearts, we ask for the gift of repentance – for a humble, contrite heart.

Prayers of the Faithful
When we repent, we allow ourselves be drawn to the light. May we allow Jesus to take our hand, to lead us out of the darkness in our lives, and into the light of his truth.

We pray for all who struggle to repent. May God's Spirit encourage them. We pray for all who refuse to repent. May God's Spirit heal their hardness of heart.

WEEK FIFTEEN – WEDNESDAY

Matthew 11:25–27 (revealing them to mere children)

Introduction to Mass
Today we hear Jesus bless the Father for revealing these things to mere children. Let us begin by joining in his prayer. Let us, God's children, bless the Father for revealing so much to us.

Prayers of the Faithful
We thank Jesus for revealing God and God's love to us. We pray that Jesus will guide us, day by day, further and further, into the mystery of God and the mystery of life and the mystery of ourselves.

'Hiding these things from the learned and clever.' We give praise for the surprising ways in which God is revealed to us – in a child, in somebody sick or suffering, in the oppressed, in the poor.

WEEK FIFTEEN – THURSDAY

Matthew 11:28–30 ('come to me')

Introduction to Mass
Jesus says to us today: Come to me and I will give you rest. Let us take up his invitation. Let us share with him our burdens and our hopes. Let us rest our souls in him.

Prayers of the Faithful
Jesus was humble of heart. May we be humble too, gentle with one another, sensitive in our words and actions. May we be close to God.

We pray for all who labour and are overburdened – all who are bowed down with burdens or expectations – all who are made to carry a heavy load.

WEEK FIFTEEN – FRIDAY

Matthew 12:1–8 (Jesus and the Sabbath)

Introduction to Mass
Today Jesus proclaims: 'here, I tell you, is something greater than the Temple'. Jesus himself is that 'something greater' – our all, our everything. We take a moment to commit ourselves once more to him.

Prayers of the Faithful
There's a sense of freedom in this gospel story. We pray that all followers of Jesus may know freedom, and the liberating effect of Jesus in their lives.

True religion is more than rituals and rules; it's about the person standing next to me. May Jesus, Lord of the Sabbath, help us to stay focused on what really matters.

WEEK FIFTEEN – SATURDAY

Matthew 12:14–21 (my beloved)

Introduction to Mass
The words spoken of Jesus today are also spoken of each one of us: 'Here is my beloved, the favourite of my soul. Let us take the words to heart, and listen as God says to each one of us: 'my beloved, the favourite of my heart'.

Prayers of the Faithful
The gospel begins with the Pharisees plotting to destroy Jesus – and ends with the nations putting their hope in him. We pray for all who hate and oppress Christianity, that their hearts may be softened.

'He will not break the crushed reed nor put out the smouldering wick.' We pray for people whose spirit is crushed or who are near to breaking point. We pray for gentleness and solidarity between people.

WEEK SIXTEEN – MONDAY

Matthew 12:38–42 (sign of Jonah)

Introduction to Mass
'Something greater' was our theme last Friday – and again today. Jesus says there is something greater than Jonah or Solomon here. Let us ponder; Jesus is the 'something greater' in our lives. We come before him.

Prayers of the Faithful
There is no need for us to look for special signs or messages. Jesus, risen from the dead, is the only sign we need. May our hearts focus on that. May we live our lives in response to that.

The only signs we should be looking for are the signs of hope, the signs of Jesus' risen life around us. May we be vigilant, and aware of the signs of new life and hope, often hidden from our sight.

WEEK SIXTEEN – TUESDAY

Matthew 12:46–50 ('who is my mother?')

Introduction to Mass
In the spirit of today's gospel, we call to mind that we are all members of the spiritual family of Jesus, the Christian family, all of us brothers and sisters in him. We pause to contemplate that for a moment.

Prayers of the Faithful
We are all mothers of Jesus if we carry him in our hearts, if we say 'Yes' to his life as Mary did. In all our relationships and interactions, may we carry Jesus in our hearts.

We are all sisters and brothers of Jesus if we do God's will, as Mary did. May the concern, the passion, the compassion that filled Jesus' heart fill our hearts also.

WEEK SIXTEEN – WEDNESDAY

Matthew 13:1–9 (the sower)

Introduction to Mass
We begin with a quiet moment. Jesus says to the crowds, 'listen, anyone who has ears'. In this Mass, we open our ears to listen to his word. We open our hearts to hear his voice.

Prayers of the Faithful
May our lives be like the rich soil. May our lives be fruitful, as we commit ourselves to our Christian calling.

May we be like the sower. May we sow seeds of hope wherever we go and however we are received. May we be a positive presence in the world. May we spread life and joy.

WEEK SIXTEEN – THURSDAY

Matthew 13:10–17 ('why do you talk in parables?')

Introduction to Mass
'Happy your eyes because they see; your ears because they hear.' With these words of Jesus, we pause to remember how happy we are to hear the good news of the gospel, and to see God's face in him.

Prayers of the Faithful
We pray for all whose hearts are hardened, whose ears are deafened, whose eyes are closed. We ask God's Spirit to give all of us a new heart; to teach us to listen; to help us to see.

We say thanks for the parables of Jesus; for his great imagination; for the stories he tells, that help us to understand. We pray for all who preach and all who teach – for the gift of great imagination.

WEEK SIXTEEN – FRIDAY

Matthew 13:18–23 (the parable of the sower explained)

Introduction to Mass
Our gospel today is about the Word of God. We think of the prayer in the Mass, 'only say the word and I will be healed'. In quiet prayer, let us open our ears to hear God's healing word.

Prayers of the Faithful
May the word of God find deep roots in all our hearts. May it become part of us. May it help us cope when troubles come our way.

'The worries of the world and the lure of riches.' May they not overpower God's word in the hearts of God's people. We pray for people who are trapped in worry, and for people who are trapped by their riches.

WEEK SIXTEEN – SATURDAY

Matthew 13:24–30 ('let them both grow')

Introduction to Mass
Jesus speaks to us today about the mysterious mix of good and evil in ourselves and in our world. As we acknowledge our own dark side, let us rejoice in the good people we are in God's eyes.

Prayers of the Faithful
The mixture of good and bad is in each of us. May our faults teach us to be humble. But most of all, may we each believe in our goodness, the goodness God sees in us, our goodness as God's own creation.

The mix of good and evil is throughout our world. May we always keep trust in the power of goodness. May people who are in the power of evil be touched and changed by the goodness of those around them.

WEEK SEVENTEEN – MONDAY

Matthew 13:31–35 (the mustard seed)

Introduction to Mass
Our gospel says that Jesus spoke in parables 'to expound things hidden since the foundation of the world'. We come into his presence now, he whose teaching holds for us the meaning of everything.

Prayers of the Faithful
May the parable of the mustard seed teach us to believe – to believe in making a beginning, however small, to believe in what we have to offer, however insignificant it feels.

May the parable of the yeast teach us to believe that when we add in our faith and our hope and our love, it can make a difference to everything. May the lives of Christians have a transforming effect on the world.

WEEK SEVENTEEN – TUESDAY

Matthew 13:36–43 (the parable of the wheat explained)

Introduction to Mass
Again today, Jesus says to the crowds, 'listen, anyone who has ears'. In this Mass, we open our ears to listen to his word. We open our hearts to hear his voice.

Prayers of the Faithful
Our gospel is about, not so much a punishing God, as a caring God, passionate about justice and right. May we grow in faith that our God will make all things right. We pray, 'your kingdom come'.

We pray for the Church in the world. We know it can fail and be part of the evil. But we pray that it will be purified, and be a great force for good, for the bringing about of God's kingdom.

WEEK SEVENTEEN – WEDNESDAY

Matthew 13:44–46 (the pearl of great price)

Introduction to Mass
Finding a treasure; there's a sense of amazement in today's gospel. We begin by opening ourselves to being amazed again by what we believe, by the good news of the gospel.

Prayers of the Faithful
'He sells everything to buy it.' May the joy of what we've been given inspire us to live a generous life, to give of ourselves gladly and willingly, to make our lives a gift for others.

We pray for all who are searching for the treasure – for a meaning in their lives, for something that really matters, for something to live for.

WEEK SEVENTEEN – THURSDAY

Matthew 13:47–53 (the dragnet)

Introduction to Mass
We come before the Lord, each of us a mix of good and bad, light and darkness. We know God sees great good in each of us. Confidently, we ask God's healing of our sins and weaknesses.

Prayers of the Faithful
Jesus is saying that our Church is a mix of saints and sinners, and to be patient. May we be humble and tolerant of one another. May we be kind. By our kindness, may we encourage each other to goodness and holiness.

'Things both old and new.' We pray for our Church in changing times. May it be creative and innovative, willing to change. And may it be faithful to all we hold dear in our tradition.

WEEK SEVENTEEN – FRIDAY

Matthew 13:54–58 ('the carpenter's son, surely?')

Introduction to Mass
'He did not work many miracles there, because of their lack of faith.' For a moment, let us ponder this gospel message. Let us open our hearts, with faith in the Lord's power to change our lives.

Prayers of the Faithful
A prophet is despised in their own country. We think gratefully of the prophets among us, pointing us to the truth. May our Church and society be open to listening, no matter where the prophetic voices come from.

Maybe Jesus was too familiar to the people in this story. We pray not to become complacent, nor to presume we know him. Lord, may we be surprised and challenged by you.

WEEK SEVENTEEN – SATURDAY

Matthew 14:1–12 (John the Baptist's death)

Introduction to Mass
The shocking death of John the Baptist is today's gospel story. We prepare to listen to it by quietly asking God to help us overcome whatever is evil or violent or false in our own hearts.

Prayers of the Faithful
The gospel invites us to pray for all throughout the world who suffer and are killed because they speak the truth. We praise God for their courage. We pray with confidence that their courage makes a difference.

We pray for all who, like Herod, are tempted by the evil intentions of others to do evil themselves. May we never lead others into temptation. May we have courage to resist the temptation of evildoing.

WEEK EIGHTEEN – MONDAY

Matthew 14:13–21 (the loaves and fishes)

Introduction to Mass
Today's gospel of the loaves and fishes focuses our minds on Jesus the bread of life. We come before him, with our soul's hunger, to be nourished by him.

Prayers of the Faithful
As we listen again to this miracle of sharing, we think of the hunger in our world, and the scandal that there is enough for all. May the Lord teach all people the miracle of sharing.

We pray for people who cannot feed themselves – people who are disabled, people who are housebound, people who are destitute. And we ask God to bless the people who care for them.

WEEK EIGHTEEN – TUESDAY

Matthew 14:22–36 (the storm on the lake)

Introduction to Mass
The disciples in our gospel are battling with a storm on the lake but Jesus is watching, and sees. Let us take a moment to sense him watching over us in our struggles and troubles.

Prayers of the Faithful
'Truly you are the Son of God.' May this faith of ours help us whenever we are afraid, like the disciples were. May it strengthen us whenever we have doubts, like Peter had.

We pray for those we know who are battling with difficulties – financial difficulties, relationship difficulties, spiritual difficulties. May they be comforted and reassured by the Lord's watching over them.

WEEK EIGHTEEN – WEDNESDAY

Matthew 15:21–28 (the Canaanite woman)

Introduction to Mass
The woman in the gospel cries to Jesus, 'Son of David, have pity on me'. We too bring before the Lord whatever is troubling us, or whatever we are worried about, trusting in his compassion.

Prayers of the Faithful
We see the faith and determination of a woman caring for her sick daughter. We think of all parents. We give thanks for their faith and their boundless love for their children.

The gospel tells us that God is not restricted to any one people – that God embraces all equally. We pray for people of different faiths. May the diversity of beliefs in our world be an enrichment to all.

WEEK EIGHTEEN – THURSDAY

Matthew 16:13–23 (who do you say I am?)

Introduction to Mass
Today we hear Jesus ask us as he asked Peter: Who do you say that I am? In the silence of our hearts, let us respond with Peter: 'You are the Christ, the Son of the living God'.

Prayers of the Faithful
'You are the Christ, the Son of the living God.' We ask for an ever deeper personal relationship with Jesus, to know his power, to know his message. We ask this, not just for ourselves, but for one another.

Jesus promises to be faithful to his Church. We ask him to reinvigorate his Church with the power of his Spirit. We pray for our Church leaders. May they be humble and inspiring.

WEEK EIGHTEEN – FRIDAY

Matthew 16:24–28 (renounce yourself)

Introduction to Mass
Each day, as if for the first time, Jesus asks us to follow him. In the quiet of our hearts, let us listen to his voice, as if for the first time, saying: 'follow me'.

Prayers of the Faithful
We thank God for the inspiration we get from others around us – people who let go, and renounce themselves – who take up their cross and follow Jesus. May we all, by our example, encourage each other.

We pray for all who find it hard to let go. May we ourselves be able to let go of what prevents us from following Jesus. May we cling to him alone.

WEEK EIGHTEEN – SATURDAY

Matthew 17:14–20 (faith as a mustard seed)

Introduction to Mass
Faith, Jesus tells us, is more than understanding, more than beliefs. Faith is trust – entrusting ourselves to him and the power of his Spirit. Let us be quiet for a moment, and entrust ourselves once more to him.

Prayers of the Faithful
We pray for a rich faith. May our trust in God help us also to believe in ourselves. May our trust in God help us to believe in one another and encourage one another.

The boy in the story suffers from fits and seizures and convulsions. We pray for all, younger and older, who suffer from a similar condition. And we pray for those who care for them.

WEEK NINETEEN – MONDAY

Matthew 17:22–27 (the half-shekel)

Introduction to Mass
Our special dignity is that we are God's children. Jesus says it's like being royalty, members of the royal family! We pause a moment to consider our dignity, the privilege of being God's family.

Prayers of the Faithful
Jesus says, 'so as not to offend these people'. May we, God's family, be aware of the effect we can have on others. May we take care not to offend, or to make things difficult for others.

When the disciples heard Jesus talking of his death, 'sadness came over them'. They did not hear him talking also of resurrection! May the joy of our resurrection faith help ease and heal whatever sadness is in our lives.

WEEK NINETEEN – TUESDAY

Matthew 18:1–5, 10, 12–14 (be like little children)

Introduction to Mass
We are to make ourselves as little as little children. In that spirit we begin by resting for a moment – resting in God's embrace, as would a child in its mother's arms, with trust and security.

Prayers of the Faithful
We pray for the 'little ones' among us – for our children, but also for all who are vulnerable, weak or defenceless. May we be a community of warmth, a community that cares and protects.

'Unless you change and become like little children.' Like the little child, or the lost sheep, we must be helpless, so as to find our help in God. May we learn to depend on God and be confident.

WEEK NINETEEN – WEDNESDAY

Matthew 18:15–20 (if your brother does something wrong)

Introduction to Mass
'Where two or three meet in my name, I am there with them.' Let us leave all else aside for a moment and focus completely on this – the risen Jesus present among us as we meet.

Prayers of the Faithful
We think for a moment of the differences we have with others. May Jesus' words encourage us to address those differences in a spirit of reconciliation – to be humble, to be positive, to be creative.

'Where two or three meet.' Whenever we come together, Christ is present. May we bring a sense of his presence to all our encounters. May this transform the quality of our interactions with one another.

WEEK NINETEEN – THURSDAY

Matthew 18:21–19:1 (forgiveness)

Introduction to Mass
'I cancelled all your debt when you appealed to me.' With these words, Jesus tells us who our God is. In our sin and weakness, we appeal to him now, knowing his boundless forgiveness.

Prayers of the Faithful
May we try to treat each other as God treats us. May we be willing to forgive – inspired by how generously God forgives us.

The story highlights the lack of forgiveness in our world. We pray that hard hearts may learn to be merciful. May all God's people realise that we are all sisters and brothers.

WEEK NINETEEN – FRIDAY

Matthew 19:3–12 (divorce)

Introduction to Mass
In the spirit of today's gospel, we begin by remembering God's faithful love. God's love for us in Christ is irrevocable and utterly reliable. We belong to God forever. We say a silent prayer of thanks.

Prayers of the Faithful
We thank God for the faithfulness and dedication that so many people experience in their marriage. And we pray for all who have been disappointed in their marriage – we pray for new hope in their lives.

We thank God for the witness of those who forego married love in their service of God's kingdom. May their faithfulness and dedication inspire others around them in their own vocation to love.

WEEK NINETEEN – SATURDAY

Matthew 19:13–15 (Jesus welcomes children)

Introduction to Mass
In our gospel, people bring little children to Jesus. We now do the same. We think of all the children we know and we bring them to Jesus. We make them part of our prayer today.

Prayers of the Faithful
Jesus takes children seriously, unlike his disciples! May we be like him and not them. May we listen to our children and respect them. May we be happy to learn from them and be enriched by them.

We pray for children who are suffering, for those who are sick, for those who live in troubled homes, for those who are unhappy or struggling in any way.

WEEK TWENTY – MONDAY

Matthew 19:16–22 (rich young man)

Introduction to Mass
The gospel story of the rich young man tells us he went away sad, unable to take the next step. We too come to the Lord, part of us willing, part of us reluctant. We ask him to look on us with love.

Prayers of the Faithful
'What more do I need to do?' We ask the Lord to show us the path – to show us the 'more' we can do – how we can enter more into discipleship. We ask for courage to take that path.

We pray for young adults like this man. May God's Spirit guide them as they seek their path in life. May their choices be inspired by true values. May God give them courage.

WEEK TWENTY – TUESDAY

Matthew 19:23–30 (for God, everything is possible)

Introduction to Mass
Peter says to Jesus: 'we have left everything and followed you'. We pause a moment to reflect on how much Jesus means to us – the place he has assumed in our hearts – how wedded we are to him.

Prayers of the Faithful
'For God everything is possible.' Grace is infinite. May we believe this with confidence. May all await, with believing hearts, for the appearing of God's grace in their lives.

'First will be last, and the last, first.' How God sees things may be different from how they appear to us. May we be slow to presume or to judge, about who is close to God or far from God.

WEEK TWENTY – WEDNESDAY

Matthew 20:1–16 (the workers in the vineyard)

Introduction to Mass
Jesus says to each of us what he says to the workers in today's gospel: 'You go to my vineyard too'. We too are called. In our hearts let us say: 'Yes, we will go; yes, we will play our part'.

Prayers of the Faithful
'Why be envious because I am generous?' God is not unfair to those who came first – but rather, generous to those who came last. May we not begrudge, but rejoice in God's love for the ones who are last and least.

'No one has hired us.' We pray, with loving hearts, for all in our society who can find no work, and for all the families that are struggling. We thank God, with grateful hearts, for the work we do have.

WEEK TWENTY – THURSDAY

Matthew 22:1–14 (the wedding feast)

Introduction to Mass
The Eucharist we celebrate is a foretaste and promise of the heavenly banquet portrayed by Jesus in today's gospel. We take a moment to remind ourselves of what it is we celebrate.

Prayers of the Faithful
Those invited 'were not interested'. So many do not know what a joy the good news of the gospel is. May we, as a Christian community, live our Christian life with a joy and vitality that connects with others.

Jesus' story is a statement of God's inclusive spirit – everyone is invited. May our community be inclusive. May we communicate welcome and acceptance.

WEEK TWENTY – FRIDAY

Matthew 22:34–40 (love God, love your neighbour)

Introduction to Mass
Jesus gives us his great teaching – to love God and love our neighbour. First, though, let us think about the greater love – God's love, the love that makes us loveable and able to love.

Prayers of the Faithful
God is love and we are made in God's image. We pray that we will become more loving day by day – giving it our heart and soul and mind – for this is the one thing that matters.

We thank God for the love we receive and for those who love us. We think of people who do not experience love in their lives. We pray for people who find it hard to love.

WEEK TWENTY – SATURDAY

Matthew 23:1–12 (you have only one Teacher)

Introduction to Mass
Today, Jesus criticises hypocrisy and calls for humility. We begin our Mass by taking his challenge to heart. We ask for the help of God's grace in our weakness.

Prayers of the Faithful
'One Master; one Father; one Teacher.' Lord, deepen our sense of equality. May none of us think themselves better than others, or less than others. May we find unity and peace in you.

'They do not practise what they preach.' May we show our faith in how we live. We pray for our Church. May it be a credible witness in society, an inspiring presence.

ORDINARY TIME

WEEK TWENTY-ONE – MONDAY

Matthew 23:13–22 (blind guides)

Introduction to Mass
The gospels of the next three days all begin with Jesus saying, 'Alas for you, Scribes and Pharisees'. Each day he is criticising false religion. We pray that his words these days will lead us to a purer practice of our religion.

Prayers of the Faithful
Jesus calls them 'blind guides'. We pray for those who lead in our Christian communities. May the Spirit enlighten the eyes of their mind, to see the right way forward, and to guide us in that way.

Jesus is talking about all that can go wrong with religion. We pray for our own Church, for new life and revitalisation, for a new and vibrant sense of what our religion is all about.

WEEK TWENTY-ONE – TUESDAY

Matthew 23:23–26 ('clean the inside')

Introduction to Mass
Again today, Jesus challenges us to a truer religion – a faith from within, from the heart. We ask him now, in the quiet of our hearts, to purify and cleanse and reform our hearts.

Prayers of the Faithful
'Straining gnats and swallowing camels.' We can miss the point in our practice of Christianity; we can become preoccupied with incidentals. Lord, may your Spirit guide us back to the heart of what matters in our faith.

'Inside and outside.' We can be taken up with the externals. Lord, may your Spirit lead us to truly interior religion. Fill our hearts with your Spirit. May our faith be heart-felt and lived from the heart.

WEEK TWENTY-ONE – WEDNESDAY

Matthew 23:27–32 (hypocrisy)

Introduction to Mass
Again today, Jesus begins, 'Alas for you, Scribes and Pharisees'. And again today, we try to take his message to heart. We pause to listen, with our hearts, to what he is asking from us in how we live our faith.

Prayers of the Faithful
'Outside and inside.' May each of us truly be who we are. May the faith in our hearts be real and sincere. May it be expressed on the outside in our honesty and sincerity.

We pray for our Church. May it never be complacent or self-satisfied. May it hear each day the Lord's call to conversion, to purification, to transformation.

WEEK TWENTY-ONE – THURSDAY

Matthew 24:42–51 (be ready)

Introduction to Mass
Our gospel tells us to stay awake for the Lord's coming. He comes to us now in this gathering, this Eucharist. Let us open our hearts to welcome him – in the Eucharist and in one another.

Prayers of the Faithful
'You do not know when your Master is coming.' God comes when we least expect. May we learn to be aware at all times, to be vigilant, to be sensitive to God's presence – to be ready to be surprised by God.

Like the dishonest servant, we sometimes regret putting off till later what we know we should do. Lord, teach us that 'now' is what matters. Grant us courage and motivation to answer your call.

WEEK TWENTY-ONE – FRIDAY

Matthew 25:1–13 (ten bridesmaids)

Introduction to Mass
Like yesterday, the gospel is about being ready for the Lord's coming. So again today, we pause to open our hearts, for he comes to us now – in the people here with us, in the Eucharist we share.

Prayers of the Faithful
Lord, grant us attentive hearts. May we be ever attentive for your coming to us – in the people we meet, in the events of our day, in the thoughts of our minds, in the feelings of our hearts.

Like the bridesmaids, we can be sensible and we can be foolish. We ask you, Lord, to bear with us in our foolishness. Stay with us when we are slow to appreciate your presence.

WEEK TWENTY-ONE – SATURDAY

Matthew 25:14–30 (the talents)

Introduction to Mass
In our Mass today, we rejoice in what God sees in each one of us. Sometimes we are afraid and we make ourselves small. So quietly, we empty our minds now, to see what God sees in us.

Prayers of the Faithful
We thank God for the unique person each of us is. May each of us here feel God's encouragement to believe in ourselves. May each of us discover what we have to offer.

We pray for all who are lacking in confidence – who think they have nothing to offer – who are afraid to put themselves forward. May we be a community of encouragement.

WEEK TWENTY-TWO – MONDAY

Luke 4:16–30 (good news)

Introduction to Mass
Today we begin our daily reading from Luke's gospel. Jesus proclaims the good news of God's all-embracing love. Quietly we ask God to cleanse our hearts of whatever prevents us from hearing the good news.

Prayers of the Faithful
The 'good news' that Jesus brings is for the poor, the captive, the blind, the downtrodden. May each of us – in our need, our poverty, our blindness – hear the good news of God's love. May we bring that love to others in their need.

'All eyes were fixed on him.' May our eyes be fixed on Jesus. As we listen to Luke's gospel over the coming weeks and months, may our ears and our spirit become ever more attuned to him.

WEEK TWENTY-TWO – TUESDAY

Luke 4:31–37 (astonishment seized them)

Introduction to Mass
Listen to the words of today's gospel, 'he made a deep impression on them … astonishment seized them'. Let us take a moment to re-connect with our own amazement and astonishment at what we believe.

Prayers of the Faithful
The story invites us to pray for anybody who is in the power of forces they cannot control, whatever they may be. May they find the help of a higher power. May God's Spirit lead them to liberation.

'His teaching made a deep impression on them.' May we all know the enrichment that comes from reading the gospels. May we take time to be fed by the daily bread of the Word of God.

WEEK TWENTY-TWO – WEDNESDAY

Luke 4:38–44 (suffering)

Introduction to Mass
In the gospel, people bring to Jesus any friends they have who are suffering. Let us do the same. We think quietly of people we know who are suffering or sick or struggling. We bring them to Jesus in our Mass.

Prayers of the Faithful
The crowds coming to Jesus remind us of so much suffering in our world. Let us think of the struggle and pain there is in everyone's life, be it greater or lesser. May we be caring people. May we be 'wounded healers'.

While so many are making demands on him, Jesus makes his way 'to a lonely place'. We pray for balance in our lives between action and prayer. May we put our faith into practice. Then may we bring that into our prayer.

WEEK TWENTY-TWO – THURSDAY

Luke 5:1–11 (call of the first disciples)

Introduction to Mass
Jesus calls his first disciples in our gospel today. It reminds us that we too are called. We reflect for a moment on that. Jesus calls me by name. Jesus calls me to be his disciple.

Prayers of the Faithful
'Leave me, Lord, I am a sinful man.' Each of us is inadequate, unworthy. But may we put our trust in God's power. May we see in ourselves what the Lord sees. May the Lord lead us to discover our strength.

'We worked hard all night and caught nothing.' We pray for people who feel their efforts are in vain. We pray for people who keep on trusting when they see no results.

WEEK TWENTY-TWO – FRIDAY

Luke 5:33–39 (new wine, fresh skins)

Introduction to Mass
The word 'new' captures today's gospel. Our God is a God who makes things new. Our God does new things. We pray silently for a moment, for whatever 'new thing' we want from God in our own lives.

Prayers of the Faithful
This gospel spoke to the early Christians of the new beginnings that faith in the risen Christ called for. As we travel the journey of faith, may we be open to change – able to let go of the old and to embrace the new.

We are all called to change for the better. We pray for all who struggle to let go of old ways. We pray for all who find it hard to let go of the darkness, and enter into the light.

WEEK TWENTY-TWO – SATURDAY

Luke 6:1–5 (master of the Sabbath)

Introduction to Mass
'The Son of Man is master of the Sabbath.' The theme of today's gospel tells us that our allegiance is not to the rules and rituals of religion, but to Christ our Lord. In the quiet of our hearts, we look upon his face and avow our love.

Prayers of the Faithful
There is an air of freedom in this incident with Jesus and his companions. May all of us, Jesus' present-day companions, know freedom, and the liberating effect of Jesus in our lives.

We pray for all Christians who are not free in their religion – all who are weighed down, who find it constricting or a thing of fear. May they find freedom in their faith.

WEEK TWENTY-THREE – MONDAY

Luke 6:6–11 ('stretch out your hand')

Introduction to Mass
When Jesus heals the man in today's gospel, he says, 'Stretch out your hand'. Now, as we gather, we come before Jesus, with our own need for healing. Let us pause a moment, to reach out to him in faith.

Prayers of the Faithful
The gospel is about people who miss the point of what religion is all about. May it not be so for us. May we not get entangled in rules and observances. May we be firmly focused on loving God and caring for other people.

Thinking of the man in the story, we thank God for the gift of our hands. We pray for people who have lost the use of their hands, or who suffer from a debilitating disease.

WEEK TWENTY-THREE – TUESDAY

Luke 6:12–19 (the twelve apostles)

Introduction to Mass
One by one, in today's gospel, we hear the names of the twelve apostles, as Jesus calls them. In the quiet of our hearts, let us listen to his voice saying our name, as he calls each one of us by name.

Prayers of the Faithful
Jesus calls the twelve – then he brings them to where the people are, who came to be cured. May we, as a Christian community, allow Jesus to take us to where there is human need, to help and to heal.

Before this crucial moment of choosing the twelve, Jesus spent the night in prayer. May all Christians, called and sent by Jesus, give time to prayer. May prayer guide us in all the critical moments of our lives.

WEEK TWENTY-THREE – WEDNESDAY

Luke 6:20–26 ('how happy are you')

Introduction to Mass
In the gospel of the beatitudes, Jesus begins, 'how happy are you'. We take a moment to reflect – whatever the ups and downs of our life – the blessing that our relationship with Jesus is to us.

Prayers of the Faithful
We pray for people who are poor, or hungry, or weeping or struggling in any way. May we grow more aware of them. May our solidarity reassure them of the Lord's infinite care for them.

We pray for those who have plenty and are comfortable. May they not lose their way. May they keep their hearts focused on what really matters.

WEEK TWENTY-THREE – THURSDAY

Luke 6:27–38 (be compassionate)

Introduction to Mass
We are listening these days to Jesus' great Sermon – Jesus challenging us to challenge ourselves, to go further in our Christian living. We ask him now to pardon our complacency and to give us a share of his spirit.

Prayers of the Faithful
Jesus' challenge feels almost superhuman. But let us focus on the core of it. May our hearts be filled with what filled Jesus' own heart – namely, the compassion of God. May all else flow from that.

We ask now for whatever divine help we need to answer Jesus' call, help to love our enemy, help not to retaliate, help to be generous, help not to judge. Lord, give us a compassionate heart like yours.

WEEK TWENTY-THREE – FRIDAY

Luke 6:39–42 (seeing clearly)

Introduction to Mass
Our gospel today is about seeing clearly. So we begin by acknowledging before the Lord how blind and short-sighted we can be. In our hearts, we ask the Lord to enlighten the eyes of our mind.

Prayers of the Faithful
May we take Jesus' message to heart. May we be humble and aware of our own imperfections. May we be slow to judge or criticise others. May we think of others as kindly as we can.

'The fully trained disciple will be like their teacher.' On our Christian journey, may we never stop learning. Every day, may we come to know Christ better, and become more and more like him.

WEEK TWENTY-THREE – SATURDAY

Luke 6:43–49 (true foundations)

Introduction to Mass
Today's gospel is about putting faith into action. To do that, we rely on God's strength and inspiration. So now, in silence, we open our hearts to divine power and divine energy.

Prayers of the Faithful
Our words flow from what fills our hearts. We ask the Lord to heal our hardness of heart – to help us weed out what is bad in our hearts – to help goodness overflow from our hearts.

What matters in the end is what we do. That is the foundation we build on. So, let us put our faith into action. May each day reveal to us new ways of expressing and living our faith.

WEEK TWENTY-FOUR – MONDAY

Luke 7:1–10 (the centurion)

Introduction to Mass
We begin our Mass by saying in our hearts the prayer that comes from today's gospel – a humble, faith-filled prayer for healing. 'Lord, I am not worthy to have you under my roof; only say the word and I shall be healed'.

Prayers of the Faithful
The centurion brings to Jesus his concern for his sick servant. We do the same. We now bring to Jesus our prayers for those we know who are sick – or for anyone we are particularly concerned about.

Jesus is astonished: 'Not even in Israel have I found faith like this'. Let us enter into Jesus' sense of wonder. Let us give thanks for the faith people show; for all the ways faith expresses itself in people's lives.

WEEK TWENTY-FOUR – TUESDAY

Luke 7:11–17 (widow of Nain)

Introduction to Mass
Our gospel is about Jesus' deep compassion for a bereaved mother. In our Mass we celebrate his deep compassion for all of us. Quietly, for a moment, we allow him to touch us in our pain or troubles.

Prayers of the Faithful
A woman who is a widow, now loses her son. We pray for all whose hearts have been broken by such loss. In their pain, may they feel Jesus' compassionate, life-giving presence.

'He felt sorry for her.' Jesus' compassion is life-giving. We pray that something of his compassion will grow within us. When we encounter suffering, may we be a life-giving presence.

WEEK TWENTY-FOUR – WEDNESDAY

Luke 7:31–35 (the Son of Man comes, eating and drinking)

Introduction to Mass
The picture today's gospel gives us is that time spent in the company of Jesus is special time, time of joy and hope. We take a moment, silently to enter into this special time with the Lord – this time of joy and hope.

Prayers of the Faithful
'A friend of tax-collectors and sinners.' May it be today as it was then. May many people find joy in the friendship of Jesus. May they find their hope restored. May the light return to their faces.

'The Son of Man comes, eating and drinking.' Time with Jesus is time for celebration. May our Eucharist always be a real celebration – a celebration of God's love for us in Christ. May we feel its joy and know its hope.

WEEK TWENTY-FOUR – THURSDAY

Luke 7:36–50 (she covered his feet with kisses)

Introduction to Mass
Every heart is full of love, but sin blocks that love in. In the spirit of today's gospel, we take a moment to become aware of God forgiving us; opening the door of our heart, releasing the love within.

Prayers of the Faithful
'She covered his feet with kisses.' The woman's gestures express the love overflowing from her heart. May Jesus' forgiveness have the same effect on us. May it release the love in our hearts.

The greatest love comes from the heart that has known forgiveness. May all God's people have a deep sense that they are forgiven. May all realise that they can be forgiven and find the path to love.

WEEK TWENTY-FOUR – FRIDAY

Luke 8:1–3 ('as well as certain women')

Introduction to Mass
In the gospel, the people who accompany Jesus are people who have been healed, people who have found forgiveness. Let us become aware that we too are forgiven, we too are healed, we too are called.

Prayers of the Faithful
The gospel tells us that Jesus' close companions included both women and men. We pray that men and women will be equally visible and equally represented in our Church, in the spirit of Jesus.

Women and men accompany Jesus in proclaiming the good news. We are also called to that mission. May we have a strong sense of accompanying Jesus, and of being accompanied by him.

WEEK TWENTY-FOUR – SATURDAY

Luke 8:4–15 (the parable of the sower)

Introduction to Mass
In the parable of the sower, Jesus says, 'listen, anyone who has ears'. In this Mass, we open our ears to listen to his word. We open our hearts to hear his voice.

Prayers of the Faithful
We take the words of the gospel as a prayer for ourselves. May we be people with a noble and generous heart – who have heard the word, who take it to ourselves, who yield a harvest through our perseverance.

May we be like the sower. May we sow seeds of hope wherever we go and however we are received. May we be a positive presence in the world. May we spread life and joy.

WEEK TWENTY-FIVE – MONDAY

Luke 8:16–18 (so that people may see the light)

Introduction to Mass
Jesus tells us to let our light shine. First, though, let us think of Jesus, who is the light of the world. Let us ask for his light to shine on us, into the darkness of our lives, into our confusion and our questions.

Prayers of the Faithful
We are not to hide our light. Lord, help us to believe in the light that shines from each of us. Give us confidence in ourselves – to be confident in what we have to offer.

May we, as a Christian community, have a strong sense of our own mission. May we not be inward-looking. May we find our enrichment in reaching out to others – with welcome, with caring, with good news.

WEEK TWENTY-FIVE – TUESDAY

Luke 8:19–21 (my mother and brothers)

Introduction to Mass
Our gospel tells us that we are Jesus' family. We are all members of the spiritual family of Jesus, the Christian family, all of us brothers and sisters in him. We pause to contemplate that for a moment.

Prayers of the Faithful
We are all mothers of Jesus if we carry him in our hearts, if we say 'Yes' to his life as Mary did. In all our relationships and interactions, may we carry Jesus in our hearts.

May we truly be sisters and brothers of Jesus by listening intently to his word and by putting it into practice in our lives.

WEEK TWENTY-FIVE – WEDNESDAY

Luke 9:1–6 (Jesus sends out the twelve)

Introduction to Mass
In today's gospel, Jesus sends out his apostles to proclaim the good news and to bring God's healing. We begin by remembering that we too are sent. We quietly ask that this Eucharist will empower us for our mission.

Prayers of the Faithful
As Jesus sends the twelve, so we pray for missionaries. We think of those who have been missionaries to us – special people who, by word or action, have brought the good news to us. We ask God to bless them.

The twelve go from house to house. We pray for all in our parishes who are engaged in the ministry of visiting people's homes. May people find in them the welcoming, listening, caring face of the Christian community.

WEEK TWENTY-FIVE – THURSDAY

Luke 9:7–9 (Herod asks about Jesus)

Introduction to Mass
In the gospel, Herod wants to know about Jesus. It invites us to think about ourselves – to ask ourselves: What do I know about Jesus? What have I come to know about him? We pause a moment to reflect.

Prayers of the Faithful
Herod wonders about Jesus. We pray for people who have heard of Jesus, but want to know more about him. May they come to know him in their hearts, and in the welcoming community of Christians.

We pray for ourselves and our relationship to Jesus. May we come to know him more and more. May we be surprised and enraptured by him. May we come closer to him each day.

WEEK TWENTY-FIVE – FRIDAY

Luke 9:18–22 ('who do you say I am?')

Introduction to Mass
We begin with a moment of silent adoration. We think of Peter's profession of faith in today's gospel. With Peter we say to Jesus: 'You are the Christ of God'.

Prayers of the Faithful
As Christians we have a deep desire that many others would come to know who Jesus is. And while we respect other beliefs and religions, we pray that many will come to know that Jesus is the Christ of God.

Though he is the Christ of God, Jesus is destined to suffer. May we accept the suffering that is part of believing – the suffering of adversity, the pain of self-giving.

WEEK TWENTY-FIVE – SATURDAY

Luke 9:43–45 (they did not understand him)

Introduction to Mass
We should take heart from today's gospel, even Jesus' original disciples found it hard to understand. We now come before the Lord with humble hearts, that he may enlighten us. Quietly we pray: Lord, that I may see.

Prayers of the Faithful
'The disciples were afraid to ask him.' Like them, we do not understand everything. May we welcome our questions and not be afraid of them. May our questions and confusion be the doorway to a richer faith.

The disciples could not understand that failure would be part of Jesus' story. In our own faith journey, may failure not discourage us. May we find in it the path to new life.

WEEK TWENTY-SIX – MONDAY

Luke 9:46–50 (the least is the one who is great)

Introduction to Mass
Jesus says, 'Anyone who welcomes me welcomes the one who sent me'. In this quiet moment, as we begin our Mass, we welcome Jesus knowing that he is God's very presence among us.

Prayers of the Faithful
'Which of them was the greatest.' Here in our Christian community, we ask the Lord to protect us from the temptations of status, from feeling superior to others, from thinking ourselves more important than others.

'Anyone who is not against you is for you.' May we appreciate it whenever and wherever people are doing good, whoever they may be. May we not put limits on where we think the Spirit is at work.

WEEK TWENTY-SIX – TUESDAY

Luke 9:51–56 (Jesus resolutely took the road)

Introduction to Mass
In today's gospel, Jesus sets his face to Jerusalem. He takes the decisive option that will lead to the cross. In silence, let us see in his decision the sign for us of God's complete commitment to us.

Prayers of the Faithful
'Jesus resolutely took the road for Jerusalem.' We ask him now to bless each one of us on our Christian journey. We ask him to give us a share of his courage and single-minded spirit.

'Jesus resolutely took the road for Jerusalem.' We pray for all who face big decisions in their lives; all who have to choose which way to go. Like Jesus, may they make their choices in a spirit of loving commitment.

WEEK TWENTY-SIX – WEDNESDAY

Luke 9:57–62 ('follow me')

Introduction to Mass
Today's gospel is about following Jesus and we are gathered here as his followers. We pause to pray for a moment for one another and for the people who encourage us in following the Lord.

Prayers of the Faithful
One person says to Jesus: 'I will follow you wherever you go'. The words are easy to say, harder to do. We pray to the Lord that we will become more resolved and committed in following him.

Jesus' words are about being committed and decisive. We pray for all who are wavering or unsure in their faith. We pray for all who are hesitant or afraid in their faith. We pray for courage for all who believe.

WEEK TWENTY-SIX – THURSDAY

Luke 10:1–12 (Jesus sends out seventy-two others)

Introduction to Mass
'The kingdom of God is very near to you.' We begin with these words of Jesus from today's gospel, telling us how near God is, how near grace is. We take a moment to let the words sink into our hearts: 'The kingdom of God is very near to you.'

Prayers of the Faithful
We pray for labourers for the harvest. We pray that more and more Christians come to a new awareness of their baptism – a new sense that they are called by name, that they are sent to do God's work.

Welcome and hospitality figure large in our gospel. We pray that they will always be to the fore throughout our Church. May our welcome and hospitality help people come to God.

WEEK TWENTY-SIX – FRIDAY

Luke 10:13–16 (repentance)

Introduction to Mass
In our gospel, Jesus reproaches those who refuse to repent. Now, in the silence of our hearts, we ask for the gift of repentance – the gift of a humble, contrite heart.

Prayers of the Faithful
When we repent, we allow ourselves be drawn to the light. May we allow Jesus to take our hand, to lead us out of the darkness in our lives, and into the light of his truth.

'Who listens to you listens to me.' Lord, grant us the gift of listening. May we be welcoming and attentive when others speak. May we hear your voice when we listen to one another.

WEEK TWENTY-SIX – SATURDAY

Luke 10:17–24 ('happy the eyes')

Introduction to Mass
'Rejoice that your names are written in heaven.' We begin by taking a moment to meditate on Jesus' words to us today. Each of our names is held in God's heart, forever.

Prayers of the Faithful
'Happy the eyes that see what you see.' May each of us appreciate how privileged we are, and how much the eyes of faith have revealed to us. May we be humble and grateful.

'The seventy-two came back rejoicing.' We pray for all who work to proclaim the gospel in our world. May they have cause for rejoicing. May we all see God's Spirit at work in what we do.

WEEK TWENTY-SEVEN – MONDAY

Luke 10:25–37 (the good Samaritan)

Introduction to Mass
In the early Church, today's gospel of the good Samaritan was interpreted to mean that Jesus is the good Samaritan and that we are the wounded one by the roadside. So now, let us take a moment to become aware of Jesus and of his healing presence with us here.

Prayers of the Faithful
We thank God for the 'good Samaritans' among us, all who go out of their way to help others. May we all share the same instinct to be compassionate, whenever we encounter another in need.

We think of the Samaritans organisation. We pray for the anonymous people they serve, people who are desperate for help and for hope.

WEEK TWENTY-SEVEN – TUESDAY

Luke 10:38–42 (Martha and Mary)

Introduction to Mass
In today's gospel, a woman named Martha welcomes Jesus into her house. Her sister Mary sits down at his feet. We now welcome Jesus into our midst. Let us sit at his feet and listen to him speak to us.

Prayers of the Faithful
May we share the active spirit of Martha. May we be active in doing good. May we welcome the Lord as he comes to us in other people. May we be mindful of others.

May we share the contemplative spirit of Mary. May we make time for the Lord in our busy lives. May the time spent with him soothe our spirits and lift our hearts.

WEEK TWENTY-SEVEN – WEDNESDAY

Luke 11:1–4 (Our Father)

Introduction to Mass
Today the disciples say to Jesus: 'teach us to pray'. Let us make that our intention in this Mass – that Jesus will teach us to pray – that he will lead us into prayer that is deeper, simpler and richer.

Prayers of the Faithful
In the spirit of Jesus' prayer, we focus ourselves on God. We pray that God's kingdom will be foremost in our hearts. Lord, may all we do each day be for the glory of your name and the coming of your kingdom.

In the spirit of Jesus' prayer, we confidently ask God's help. May God nourish and sustain us daily. May God give us the spirit of forgiveness. May God protect us from evil.

WEEK TWENTY-SEVEN – THURSDAY

Luke 11:5–13 (persistent prayer)

Introduction to Mass
Today, Jesus tells us that the Father always gives the Holy Spirit to those who ask. We open our hearts now, with whatever preoccupies our heart at the moment. We open ourselves to the gift of God's Holy Spirit.

Prayers of the Faithful
God knows our needs before ever we pray, and knows them better than we do. We ask God to teach us and enlighten us, to show us what to pray for, to lead us to our deepest desires.

We ask God for the gift of persistence in prayer. May we keep on looking out for how God is answering our prayers, in ways we might never have expected. May we allow God to surprise us.

WEEK TWENTY-SEVEN – FRIDAY

Luke 11:15–26 (by the finger of God)

Introduction to Mass
Our gospel tells us that, in Jesus, God's kingdom has come near to us. Let us look no further than him. Let us rest our hearts in Jesus, in whom all the fulness of God was pleased to dwell.

Prayers of the Faithful
This gospel is about recognising Jesus and where he comes from. We pray that many people will be drawn by his words and attracted by his deeds – that many will recognise in him the power and presence of God.

Jesus' story of the 'seven other spirits' warns us not to be complacent. May we keep challenging ourselves in our Christian living. May we keep pushing forward, lest we start slipping backwards.

WEEK TWENTY-SEVEN – SATURDAY

Luke 11:27–28 ('still happier those')

Introduction to Mass
'Happier those who hear the word of God and keep it.' The words of today's gospel invite us into a quiet prayer of thanksgiving, for the grace we experience through hearing and living the gospel.

Prayers of the Faithful
Mary carried Jesus in her womb, but also in her heart. May we be like Mary. May we take God's Word to heart. May we carry Jesus in our heart. May we say 'Yes' to his life growing within us.

As we carry Jesus in our hearts, may we also give birth to Jesus in our lives. May his life radiate from us. May his hope and compassion pour forth from us and touch the lives of others.

WEEK TWENTY-EIGHT – MONDAY

Luke 11:29–32 (the sign of Jonah)

Introduction to Mass
The theme of our gospel is: 'something greater'. Jesus says there is something greater than Jonah or Solomon here. Jesus is that 'something greater' in our lives. Quietly, we come before him.

Prayers of the Faithful
There is no need for us to look for special signs or messages. Jesus, risen from the dead, is the only sign we need. May our hearts focus on that. May we live our lives in response to that.

The only signs we should be looking for are the signs of hope, the signs of Jesus' risen life around us. May we be vigilant and aware of the signs of new life and hope, often hidden from our sight.

WEEK TWENTY-EIGHT – TUESDAY

Luke 11:37–41 (give alms from what you have)

Introduction to Mass
For Jesus, the heart is what matters. In the spirit of today's gospel, we open ourselves to the Lord, who sees our heart. We ask the Lord to cleanse our heart; to lift our heart; to give us new heart.

Prayers of the Faithful
Jesus talks of external actions and inner attitudes. We pray for inner integrity. May our attitudes be kind and positive. May our motives be pure and loving. May all we do flow from that.

'Give alms from what you have.' Jesus is saying that the best gift is the gift of ourselves. May we put ourselves into all our giving. May we give willingly of our time, our attention, our love.

WEEK TWENTY-EIGHT – WEDNESDAY

Luke 11:42–46 ('Alas for you Pharisees')

Introduction to Mass
In today's gospel, Jesus points out how people can practise their religion in a false way. We come into his presence now with a humble prayer; Lord, help us to practise our faith in an ever more genuine way.

Prayers of the Faithful
'Justice and the love of God.' May we not overlook what really matters in religion. May nothing distract us. May we grow more focused each day on justice and the love of God.

'Burdens that are unendurable.' We pray for people who feel that the Church places huge burdens on them. We pray for a Church that is sensitive to what is going on in people's lives.

WEEK TWENTY-EIGHT – THURSDAY

Luke 11:47–54 ('Alas for you lawyers')

Introduction to Mass
Our gospel sees Jesus continue to criticise the leaders of his own Jewish religion. In that same spirit, we begin by asking the Lord to forgive our Church for its shortcomings and to help it repent of its failings.

Prayers of the Faithful
Listening to Jesus' sharp attack on the religious leaders, we pray for the leaders in our Church. May they always be true to what really matters in our religion. May they be people of integrity and inspiration.

Jesus makes his criticism in a spirit of loyalty. May each of us have the gift of critical loyalty. May we be alert to the shortcomings of our Church, while staying faithful to its ideals.

WEEK TWENTY-EIGHT – FRIDAY

Luke 12:1–7 (every hair on your head)

Introduction to Mass
We begin by taking into our hearts the words of Jesus in the gospel. He says to each of us personally: 'No one is forgotten in God's sight. Why, every hair on your head has been counted. There is no need to be afraid'.

Prayers of the Faithful
Twice today Jesus says, 'do not be afraid'. May God, who is always with us, change our fear to trust and confidence. And we reach out in prayer to think of people who are gripped by fear.

Jesus says that the only one we need fear is God. Let us heed his prayer. May our only fear be the fear of ever distancing ourselves from such an infinitely caring God.

WEEK TWENTY-EIGHT – SATURDAY

Luke 12:8–12 (the Spirit will teach you)

Introduction to Mass
Jesus tells us not to worry, that the Spirit will teach us what to say. So let us enter into silence for a moment. Let us allow the Spirit to utter our prayers, to bring our deepest needs to God the Father.

Prayers of the Faithful
By gathering here, we are openly declaring ourselves for Jesus. May we feel God's Spirit in the support of one another. May that give us confidence to witness to Jesus wherever we go.

The sin 'that will not be forgiven' most likely means the complete rejection of God's love in Christ. We pray with confidence, that this will be true of nobody. We pray that every heart, however hard, contains some opening to God.

WEEK TWENTY-NINE – MONDAY

Luke 12:13–21 (rich in the sight of God)

Introduction to Mass
We begin by taking to heart what Jesus teaches in today's gospel – that our desire for things can take over and can take the place of God in our lives. In the quiet of our hearts, we allow his words to challenge us.

Prayers of the Faithful
Jesus teaches us what really matters in life. May we take his words to heart and learn how to live well. May we spend our energy on what is of lasting value – such as solidarity and truth, integrity and generosity.

We thank God for the good things of life. May we enjoy them without becoming enslaved to pleasures and possessions. May God's grace help us conquer the greed in ourselves and in our world.

WEEK TWENTY-NINE – TUESDAY

Luke 12:35–38 (be ready)

Introduction to Mass
In the spirit of today's gospel, we take a quiet moment as we begin. We ready ourselves for Jesus' coming. We open the door of our hearts as he comes and knocks.

Prayers of the Faithful
Be 'ready to open the door'. The Lord can come to us in any moment. So we pray for the gift of living in the present moment, ready for the grace of his presence, ready to recognise and respond.

We pray for people who are preoccupied – so busy, or anxious, or taken up with things that they cannot live life in the present. We pray for the grace of letting go of preoccupations and becoming aware.

WEEK TWENTY-NINE – WEDNESDAY

Luke 12:39–48 (the faithful servant)

Introduction to Mass
Today, as he did yesterday, Jesus tells us to be ready. So again today, we take a quiet moment to make ourselves ready for his coming. We leave aside distractions and temptations. We wait for the Lord.

Prayers of the Faithful
Sometimes, like the servant, we postpone responding to God's call. Lord, grant us a greater sense of urgency. Help us see that what matters is 'here and now' – to see that 'here and now' is where you are.

The gospel is partly about leaders in the community living up to their responsibility. So we pray for leaders in our Church. May they not be careless, but serious and intent in fulfilling their role.

WEEK TWENTY-NINE – THURSDAY

Luke 12:49–53 ('I have come to bring fire')

Introduction to Mass
In today's gospel Jesus says, 'I have come to bring fire to the earth'. There is an ancient Christian writing which says, 'to be near Jesus is to be near the fire'. So we draw near to him now, that he might re-ignite the fire in our hearts.

Prayers of the Faithful
Jesus' words sound harsh, divisive. But it's to make a point – that there is struggle involved in being his disciples. May we be single-minded in our commitment. May he help us be faithful and persevering.

Jesus came to bring fire to the earth. May the Holy Spirit rekindle that fire in our Church. May our Church be alive with the very passion of Jesus.

WEEK TWENTY-NINE – FRIDAY

Luke 12:54–59 (how to interpret these times)

Introduction to Mass
In the spirit of today's gospel, we begin with a moment of silent reflection. We think of the things that are going on in our life. We ask God's Spirit to help us interpret them well and to find the signs of hope.

Prayers of the Faithful
'How to interpret these times.' We pray that the Spirit will work in our Church, as it seeks to throw light on the times we live in. May our Church help us to see the signs of hope in our midst.

The gospel talks about people in conflict. So we think of the differences we have with other people. May we do all we can to settle our differences. May we think of others as kindly as we can.

WEEK TWENTY-NINE – SATURDAY

Luke 13:1–9 (unless you repent)

Introduction to Mass
The refrain of Jesus in today's gospel is: 'unless you repent'. May we see this quiet moment now as a God-given opportunity. May we allow ourselves to be drawn by the Lord out of the darkness, into the light.

Prayers of the Faithful
The man says, 'leave it one more year'. The good news of the gospel is that there is always another chance. We pray that nobody will feel condemned or give up. May all believe in the possibility of new beginnings.

We ask God for the grace of repentance. May we be humble enough to acknowledge our weakness. May we be open enough to see our sins and failings. May we be courageous enough to repent.

WEEK THIRTY – MONDAY

Luke 13:10–17 ('bound these eighteen years')

Introduction to Mass
In our gospel today, Jesus heals a woman on the Sabbath. At the heart of our religion is this: God's care, God's healing, for each person in their need. Quietly we bring to the Lord our own need to be healed.

Prayers of the Faithful
Eighteen years is a long time. We pray for people who have been suffering or carrying a cross for many years. May God's Spirit be with them in their patience and endurance.

The woman was 'bent double'. We pray for people who are physically disabled, and all whose movement is impaired. May the Lord's Spirit keep their spirit strong.

WEEK THIRTY – TUESDAY

Luke 13:18–21 (what is the kingdom of God like?)

Introduction to Mass
Jesus brings something new to our lives. Today's gospel compares it to yeast mixed into the dough. Let us reflect a moment on what Jesus brings to our lives, and how it changes everything.

Prayers of the Faithful
May the parable of the mustard seed teach us to believe; to believe in making a beginning, however small, to believe in what we have to offer, however insignificant it feels.

May the parable of the yeast teach us to believe that, when we add in our faith and our hope and our love, it can make a difference to everything. May the lives of Christians have a transforming effect on the world.

WEEK THIRTY – WEDNESDAY

Luke 13:22–30 (from east and west, north and south)

Introduction to Mass
In our gospel there is a picture of people, from east and west, north and south, coming to the feast in the kingdom of God. Let us make our Mass today a prayer for all God's people. Let us bring all – east and west, north and south – into our prayer.

Prayers of the Faithful
The gospel teaches that God's love is universal, not confined to any special group or religion. May we all have a generous appreciation for the dignity of all God's people – all of them called, all of them cherished by God.

Today's gospel holds a warning, not to become smug or complacent in our faith. May we not be presumptuous or take our salvation for granted. May we hear God's call anew each day.

WEEK THIRTY – THURSDAY

Luke 13:31–35 ('I must go on')

Introduction to Mass
'Blessings on him who comes in the name of the Lord.' We begin by quietly focusing on Jesus' words. We leave all distractions aside. We welcome him who comes into our midst and into our hearts.

Prayers of the Faithful
Jesus says, 'I must go on'. He will not be diverted from his course. We ask for a share of Jesus' Spirit. May we let nothing interfere with following his call. May nothing distract or deflect us.

As Jesus grieves for Jerusalem, so we pray for our world today, so often unreceptive to God's Word. We pray for a new opening in human hearts to the good news of the gospel.

WEEK THIRTY – FRIDAY

Luke 14:1–6 (healing on the Sabbath)

Introduction to Mass
We see in today's gospel how Jesus' first concern is always for people, for the well-being of God's people. This encourages us now to bring our own needs to him, knowing how much he cares.

Prayers of the Faithful
Jesus' healing on the Sabbath sends out a message; that what comes first in religion is people. May we, and all Christians, make it our priority concern to care for other people in their need.

We pray for particular people we know who are unwell – people who are struggling with some health problem. We reach out in our prayer, to touch them with our care.

WEEK THIRTY – SATURDAY

Luke 14:1, 7–11 (places of honour)

Introduction to Mass
In Jesus' story in today's gospel, he says that there are no places of honour at the Lord's table. Let us take that to heart as we gather today. For Jesus, our host, we are all equally honoured, all equally welcome.

Prayers of the Faithful
We pray for a changed world, where dignity is more important than status. May we not be so concerned with importance or status. May we be concerned instead that all people are equally welcome and dignified.

Even though all are equal, we pray for those who are most in need. May they have a special place in our hearts, as they do in God's. We pray for those whose pain or need is greatest.

WEEK THIRTY-ONE – MONDAY

Luke 14:12–14 ('invite the poor')

Introduction to Mass
Today's gospel tells us about the Eucharist. It is God's own meal, to which we are invited. We have not earned it; it is pure grace. God simply wants us to come and share in the divine life. In the quiet of our hearts we say 'Yes' to God's invitation.

Prayers of the Faithful
May we, who share in this Eucharistic meal, have a special care for the poor and all who are anyway disadvantaged. May we go out of our way to make them feel welcome.

The gospel says to give without thought of reward. When we give, may we always be thinking of the good of the other person. May we be other-centred more than self-centred in our concern.

WEEK THIRTY-ONE – TUESDAY

Luke 14:15–24 (a great banquet)

Introduction to Mass
The Eucharist we celebrate is a foretaste of the heavenly banquet portrayed by Jesus in today's gospel. We pause a moment to remind ourselves how great an invitation we have received.

Prayers of the Faithful
'All started to make excuses.' We pray that the concerns and worries of life will not prevent people appreciating what God is offering to them in Christ.

'Go out to the open roads.' God's invitation is for all humanity. May we, as a Christian community, reflect the inclusiveness of God's embrace. May we communicate welcome to all.

WEEK THIRTY-ONE – WEDNESDAY

Luke 14:25–33 (work out the cost)

Introduction to Mass
Jesus calls us to be his disciples, and to renounce whatever stands in the way of following him. We each can ask ourselves: what is preventing me from following him? And we ask for strength and courage.

Prayers of the Faithful
'Sit down and work out the cost.' May none of us take lightly our following of Christ. May we be realistic in measuring what it demands of us – and courageous in responding.

We pray for women and men in religious life. Their vocation is to encourage us all in the following of Christ. May they be faithful and inspiring witnesses.

WEEK THIRTY-ONE – THURSDAY

Luke 15:1–10 (lost sheep, lost coin)

Introduction to Mass
'This man', the Pharisees say in our gospel, 'welcomes sinners and eats with them'. Let us take a moment to rejoice and lift up our hearts. For Jesus now welcomes us, who are sinners. He sits down and eats with us.

Prayers of the Faithful
May we share God's joy in welcoming sinners. May we rejoice when somebody changes for the better. May we be generous, and not begrudging, when another person repents.

May our Church be like our God – welcoming rather than judging, including rather than excluding. May people who have failed, or people who are struggling, find in our Church a welcoming home.

WEEK THIRTY-ONE – FRIDAY

Luke 16:1–8 (the astute steward)

Introduction to Mass
Today's gospel tells of a steward who was wasteful with his master's property. Similarly, we can be wasteful or irresponsible in our Christian calling. So we turn to the Lord with repentant hearts.

Prayers of the Faithful
Jesus is praising the steward for his astuteness, not for his dishonesty. As disciples of Jesus, may we too be astute. May we be shrewd and constructive in the decisions we have to make.

We pray for people who are in debt and struggling to repay. We think of all who are going through financial hardships. We hope that people help each other to cope and not lose heart.

WEEK THIRTY-ONE – SATURDAY

Luke 16:9–15 (use of money)

Introduction to Mass
In today's gospel it says: 'God knows your hearts'. Let us rest with this thought for a moment. God sees what is in our hearts – all the rising and falling of our spirit, our strengths and our failings. And God loves us.

Prayers of the Faithful
The gospel tells us to use money well. We pray for those who have more of the world's wealth. May they be generous in sharing with the needy. We pray that we will all grow in the spirit of sharing.

We pray that we will not be enslaved by the things of the world, by power or possessions or pleasure. May our love for God teach us to enjoy the things of the world well and wisely.

WEEK THIRTY-TWO – MONDAY

Luke 17:1–6 (increase our faith)

Introduction to Mass
Jesus tells us: 'Obstacles are sure to come'. Each day brings spiritual struggles and temptations. We reflect for a moment on the obstacles we face. We turn to Jesus, our companion on the journey.

Prayers of the Faithful
We listen to Jesus encouraging us to forgive. We think of those whom we find it hard to forgive. We think of people who cannot forgive. Lord, increase in all of us the desire to be forgiving.

With the apostles, we pray: 'Lord, increase our faith'. Give us more trust; reassure us in our doubt. Give us more courage; help conquer our fear.

WEEK THIRTY-TWO – TUESDAY

Luke 17:7–10 (we are merely servants)

Introduction to Mass
We begin by thinking about Jesus' words today: 'We are merely servants; we have done no more than our duty'. We bring to mind our own duties in life. Before the Lord, we renew our dedication.

Prayers of the Faithful
We pray for all who faithfully fulfil their duties, day by day – even though it may be tiring or trying or unnoticed or unrewarding. Bless them, Lord, and encourage them.

We ask the Lord to help us keep going when what we do is not noticed or appreciated. Help us to keep doing our best. Help us to be faithful servants.

WEEK THIRTY-TWO – WEDNESDAY

Luke 17:11–19 (ten lepers)

Introduction to Mass
Our gospel is the story of the ten lepers. Let us see ourselves in the one who came back to Jesus. Let us come to Jesus in this Eucharist, to give thanks and praise for all that God does for us.

Prayers of the Faithful
Thinking of the other nine, we hope that all God's people will have the gift of a thankful heart. May all appreciate the gift that is life. May all come to acknowledge God, the giver of the gift.

Somebody said, 'It's not happiness that makes you grateful; it's gratitude that makes you happy'. May we Christians have thankful hearts. May that help us see the grace that is everywhere.

WEEK THIRTY-TWO – THURSDAY

Luke 17:20–25 (the kingdom of God is among you)

Introduction to Mass
'The kingdom of God is among you.' We stay with Jesus' words for a moment. Let us stop and ask: where is God in my life? Where is God present, and I have not noticed?

Prayers of the Faithful
'The kingdom of God is among you.' We pray for the gift of awareness, to see how God is present in people and in situations. May we learn to stop and to notice.

'The Son of Man must suffer.' We too know that the pains and difficulties of life cannot be avoided. We ask for hearts, strong with hope, to deal with troubles when they come.

WEEK THIRTY-TWO – FRIDAY

Luke 17:26–37 ('when the day comes')

Introduction to Mass
Today's gospel reminds us that none of us knows when the end will come. The thought invites us, as we begin our Mass, to rest our anxious hearts in the Lord's embrace and to know his peace.

Prayers of the Faithful
Jesus' words bring to mind how death can just come out of nowhere. We think of people who have died suddenly. We pray for people who have to cope with a sudden death.

We know not the day nor the hour. Lord, help us to live life in the present, to put our hearts into what we do, to live each day and each moment as a special moment of grace.

WEEK THIRTY-TWO – SATURDAY

Luke 18:1–8 (never lose heart)

Introduction to Mass
Today Jesus tells us 'never to lose heart'. We take his words to heart. We think quietly of what is weighing us down or discouraging us. We share our tears with our God, who is passionately on our side.

Prayers of the Faithful
We think of people who are looking for justice and for their just rights. May they not lose heart. May justice be done.

We pray for all who cry to God, day and night. May they find God's help in their cries. May they not lose heart.

WEEK THIRTY-THREE – MONDAY

Luke 18:35–43 (a blind man)

Introduction to Mass
In today's gospel, Jesus asks the blind man who cries out to him: 'What do you want me to do for you?' In the quiet of our hearts, Jesus asks each of us the same question: 'What do you want me to do for you?'

Prayers of the Faithful
'They told him that Jesus the Nazarene was passing by.' May we have eyes to see when Jesus is passing by. May we take time to notice him coming towards us in people who come our way.

We pray for people who are blind, or whose vision is impaired or failing. We ask God to bless those who work with and for blind people. May all have courage and encouragement.

WEEK THIRTY-THREE – TUESDAY

Luke 19:1–10 (Zacchaeus)

Introduction to Mass
Jesus says to each of us what he says to Zacchaeus: 'I must stay at your house today'. And we do what Zacchaeus did – we welcome him joyfully into the house of our heart.

Prayers of the Faithful
We pray for people who, like Zacchaeus, are making a determined effort to change for the better. May we rejoice, and not complain, when God is at work in people's hearts.

We live in a world of greed and ill-gotten wealth. May human hearts be charged with feelings of generosity and solidarity, just as happened Zacchaeus.

WEEK THIRTY-THREE – WEDNESDAY

Luke 19:11–28 (the ten pounds)

Introduction to Mass
The gospel today says that each of us, in our time on earth, has been given a special task by the Lord. We take a moment to think about what we've come to know about our own special calling. And maybe also, what we still are trying to understand.

Prayers of the Faithful
We thank God for the unique person each of us is. May each one here feel God's encouragement. May we believe in ourselves. May each of us discover what we have to offer.

We pray for all who are lacking in confidence, who think they have nothing to offer, who are afraid to put themselves forward. May we be a community of encouragement.

WEEK THIRTY-THREE – THURSDAY

Luke 19:41–44 (Jesus weeps over Jerusalem)

Introduction to Mass
Jesus, in today's gospel, weeps over Jerusalem. In the same spirit, we weep now in our hearts, over the graces we have missed. We bring our tears to the God of new beginnings.

Prayers of the Faithful
'If you had only understood the message of peace.' We, and all God's people, have a huge desire for inner peace. May we come to know what makes for our peace. May we find peace in our hearts.

'You did not recognise your opportunity.' We know graces can be missed. May each of us be alive to God's offer. May we be able to recognise the opportunities we are given.

WEEK THIRTY-THREE – FRIDAY

Luke 19:45–48 (Jesus clears the temple)

Introduction to Mass
In the gospel today, Jesus says, 'My house will be a house of prayer'. We now take pause to be quiet. We come into this place of prayer with reverent hearts. We come into the Lord's presence.

Prayers of the Faithful
The people 'hung onto Jesus' words'. May this be true of each of us. Each day, may we be fascinated again by the Lord. Each day, may we find new meaning in what he says.

'My house will be called a house of prayer.' We thank God for this place of prayer where we come to worship. May many others feel its welcome, and come to find the presence and peace of God here.

WEEK THIRTY-THREE – SATURDAY

Luke 20:27–40 (God of the living)

Introduction to Mass
Today's gospel invites us to believe in the life-giving power of God. So now, for a quiet moment, whatever our situation, whatever our need, we open ourselves to God's power to breathe new life in us.

Prayers of the Faithful
God of the living, may faith in Christ's resurrection give people courage in adversity and suffering. Help us witness to the resurrection by bringing hope into one another's lives.

God of the living, we entrust our dead brothers and sisters to you. We think of them now. Fill them, when they awake, with the sight of your glory.

WEEK THIRTY-FOUR – MONDAY

Luke 21:1–4 (the poor widow)

Introduction to Mass
In our gospel story of the poor widow, Jesus praises her generous spirit. We begin by thinking of the generosity of God's own self-giving in Christ – for which this Eucharist is our thanksgiving.

Prayers of the Faithful
We pray for people who feel that they have little to give. May they come to see how rich they are. May we all find joy in giving ourselves and giving our time.

We pray for those among us who are widowed. May they go on hearing the call to love. May they continue to enrich others with their love.

WEEK THIRTY-FOUR – TUESDAY

Luke 21:5–11 (the end is not so soon)

Introduction to Mass
Jesus is described in the bible as the anchor for our souls. He gives us stability amid all the tribulations talked of in today's gospel. Quietly now, we rest our souls in him.

Prayers of the Faithful
There's a sense in this gospel of how all things must pass. May we place our trust in what is of lasting value. In all passing things, may people seek God; may people seek truth and love.

Jesus talks of wars and earthquakes and plagues and famine. We reach out in our prayer to people across the world who are suffering in any such disasters.

WEEK THIRTY-FOUR – WEDNESDAY

Luke 21:12–19 (endurance)

Introduction to Mass
In our gospel Jesus shows appreciation of how difficult it can be to follow him in the world. And he assures us that we are not alone. We pause now to feel the strength of his presence.

Prayers of the Faithful
We pray for all who bear witness to the gospel, for all who bear witness to the truth, for all who bear witness to justice. We pray for the gift of endurance.

May God's Spirit give us wisdom and eloquence. May we be strong in standing up for our beliefs. We pray for the gift of endurance.

WEEK THIRTY-FOUR – THURSDAY

Luke 21:20–28 (your liberation is near at hand)

Introduction to Mass
The gospel talks of all kinds of cataclysmic events to occur before the Son of Man returns. We know, though, that the Lord comes to us each day, in all our troubles. Let us silently welcome him now.

Prayers of the Faithful
'Your liberation is near at hand.' We pray for all who are oppressed in any way. We pray for all who are longing for liberation. With the help of God's Spirit, may their hope stay alive.

We think of all the violence and vengeance in the world; all the fear and misery that people endure. May the spirit of solidarity grow strong within us. May each of us be a peace-maker.

WEEK THIRTY-FOUR – FRIDAY

Luke 21:29–33 ('my words will never pass away')

Introduction to Mass
'Heaven and earth will pass away, but my words will never pass away.' Jesus' words to us today invite us to think of him now, as the foundation of our lives, always with us, our rock and our security.

Prayers of the Faithful
Lord, give us eyes to see when your kingdom is near. Give us eyes to see you present during the day. Give us eyes to see you at work in the world.

Jesus' greatest word is 'love'. We thank God that this word will never pass away. We thank God that the love we know in this life will live for ever and never die.

WEEK THIRTY-FOUR – SATURDAY

Luke 21:34–36 (stay awake)

Introduction to Mass
As Christians, we are called to be alert and vigilant. 'Stay awake!' Jesus says in todays' gospel. So let us enter into a moment of awareness – to become aware of what God is saying to us in our lives.

Prayers of the Faithful
Jesus says, 'watch yourselves'. We pray for one another, that we will not become careless or complacent in our Christian living. May we take our calling with new seriousness each day.

Jesus says, 'pray for the strength to survive all that is going to happen'. We pray for anybody we know who is facing impending tragedy, hardship or disaster. May the Lord give them strength to survive.

Feasts

CONVERSION OF PAUL

(25 January)

Introduction to Mass
On this feast, we thank God for the difference Paul's conversion made to the early history of Christianity. We begin by opening ourselves to conversion – to letting God transform our hearts.

Prayers of the Faithful
Conversion means turning – turning towards the light, being transformed, being changed for the better. Usually it's much more slow and gradual than Paul's, but no less real. We pray for our own conversion. May we believe in our capacity to be transformed. May we allow God to lead us.

We pray for people we know who are struggling with change, people who are trying to change for the better, people who are unable to let go. May they find God's support in our support.

TIMOTHY AND TITUS

(26 January)

Introduction to Mass
Timothy and Titus were two of Paul's closest companions and co-workers. They gave him great support. We begin by quietly thanking God for the people who support us in our Christian calling.

Prayers of the Faithful
Support and encouragement are so important to all of us. We pray for those who are leaders in our Christian community. May they draw strength from our support and encouragement.

We pray for people who work behind the scenes, offering invisible support. We thank God for people who do so much to help others complete their work or perform their ministry.

THOMAS AQUINAS

(28 January)

Introduction to Mass
We thank God today for Thomas, perhaps Christianity's greatest ever theologian, and for the influence his thinking and writing have had. We pause to thank God for what we ourselves have come to understand about what we believe.

Prayers of the Faithful
We pray for all who, like Thomas, try to make Christian faith relevant to the world we live in. We pray for all theologians, who try to make Christianity meaningful to our world today.

We pray that all Christians will grow in their understanding of their faith. May God's Spirit enlighten us when we have questions, reassure us when we have doubts and guide us when we are confused.

BRIGID

(1 February)

Introduction to Mass
Brigid was a founding figure of faith in Ireland. So today is a celebration of the faith we treasure, our tradition and our inheritance. We pause for a moment in quiet gratitude for Brigid and for our faith.

Prayers of the Faithful
We thank God for Brigid's leadership in the history of Irish Christianity. We pray for all women who give Christian leadership in our parishes, in our families, in the wider Church.

We pray St Brigid's blessing: May no fire, no flame burn us. May no lake, no sea drown us. May no sword, no spear wound us. May no king, no chief insult us. May all the birds sing for us. May all the cattle low for us. May all the insects buzz for us. May the angels of God always protect us.

PRESENTATION OF THE LORD

(2 February)

Introduction to Mass
Today we celebrate Christ the light of the world and we recall the day when the child Jesus was presented in the temple. We begin by turning to Christ our light and presenting ourselves to him.

Prayers of the Faithful
We pray that we may allow ourselves to be drawn to the light that is Christ. May we present ourselves to God. May Christ make of us an everlasting gift to God.

Today is World Day for Consecrated Life. We pray for women and men in religious life in different congregations. May they be a light to the world.

BLAISE

(3 February)

Introduction to Mass
We begin with a quiet moment. Today the minister will touch our throats and bless them. Let it remind us of how God comes near and touches each of us with healing love.

Prayers of the Faithful
Before we have the blessing of throats, we pray for people who are suffering with diseases or ailments of the throat. May this day's blessing give them support and encouragement.

Before the blessing, we pray for health of mind and body for all gathered here. May this blessing teach us to value our health and encourage us to take care of our health.

OUR LADY OF LOURDES

(11 February)

Introduction to Mass
This day in 1858, Our Lady appeared to Bernadette. Now also, this day is World Day of the Sick. We pause to say a quiet prayer of thanks for Lourdes and to bring into our prayer those we know who are sick.

Prayers of the Faithful
We pray for all who are sick, in mind or body, younger or older. We pray for all who are trying to come to terms with their condition. May those who are sick be a grace and a light to others.

As we thank God for the blessings of Lourdes, we pray that its spirit will fill our homes and our community – its spirit of mutual support, of prayer, of healing, of hope.

CYRIL AND METHODIUS/VALENTINE'S DAY

(14 February)

Introduction to Mass
We thank God for these brothers from the ninth century, who brought the gospel to the Slavic peoples. And, of course, this is Valentine's day, so we pause to praise God for the gift of love.

Prayers of the Faithful
On this feast we pray for the people of Eastern Europe. We think especially of those from Eastern Europe who are now living in Ireland. May they feel welcome. May they enrich our society.

On Saint Valentine's day, we thank God for love in our lives. We pray for all who have recently found somebody to love and be loved by. We pray for all who are searching for love. We pray for all who have lost a loved one. May we all grow in love.

CHAIR OF PETER

(22 February)

Introduction to Mass
Today's feast is about Peter rather than the chair! It's about his presiding over the Church as its first leader. We begin with a quiet moment of prayer.

Prayers of the Faithful
Today we honour Peter, first bishop of Rome. We pray for his successor, our Pope. May God bless and inspire him as he leads the Church.

We pray for all who are leaders in our local church. May they lead in a spirit of service. May God's Spirit renew their spirit and ignite their enthusiasm.

PATRICK

(17 March)

Introduction to Mass
Today is a day for giving thanks to God for our faith – our inheritance from generations gone before us, our tradition of faith in Ireland, our sense of belonging and being part of it. We pause for a moment in a quiet prayer of thanks.

Prayers of the Faithful
We thank God for all – parents and teachers, witnesses and friends – who have contributed to the shaping of our own faith. May God bless them.

We pray for friends and relatives who are living in other parts of the world. May the Lord guide and protect them. May they be a blessing to those around them.

JOSEPH

(19 March)

Introduction to Mass
God is mother; God is father. On today's feast of St Joseph, we turn to God our father, the rock who saves us, the answer to all our prayers.

Prayers of the Faithful
We pray for trust in the Lord, like Joseph. May we not be afraid when God moves in new and unfamiliar ways in our lives.

We pray for all fathers and all father figures. We ask God to bless them with Joseph's integrity and Joseph's care.

ANNUNCIATION

(25 March)

Introduction to Mass
We begin our celebration by making Mary's words, and Mary's spirit of openness, our own. In quiet prayer we come before the Lord saying, 'Here I am, Lord'.

Prayers of the Faithful
The angel said, 'Rejoice, so highly favoured!' Like Mary, may we feel God's favour. May we be happy that God is with us.

The angel said, 'You are to conceive'. Like Mary, may we say 'Yes'. May we welcome Christ into our hearts and lives. May we carry Christ wherever we go.

MARK, EVANGELIST

(25 April)

Introduction to Mass
Mark is the author of one of the four gospels. For a moment, we ponder in our hearts the difference the good news of the gospel has made to our lives.

Prayers of the Faithful
'Go out to the whole world, proclaim the good news.' May we, who hear the good news, also proclaim the good news. May our speech be filled with hope and joy. May our actions be filled with compassion and integrity.

We thank God for the gospel of Mark, for the unique ways in which Mark unveils to us the mystery of Christ. May the words of the gospel sink deep in our hearts.

CATHERINE OF SIENA

(29 April)

Introduction to Mass
As we celebrate this feast, we begin by taking into our hearts the words of Jesus in today's gospel: 'Come to me, all you who labour and are overburdened, and I will give you rest'.

Prayers of the Faithful
We thank God for the gift of Catherine of Siena, a young woman with a deep experience of God. We pray for young women and young adults today. May they have a deep experience of God in their lives.

On this feast we pray for Dominican sisters, who live their lives inspired by Catherine of Siena. May this feast be a blessing for them, renewing their energy and commitment.

JOSEPH THE WORKER

(1 May)

Introduction to Mass
When we think of 'work' today, let us think of what we do in our families as well as in our factories. Let us think of time spent studying as well as time in the office. Let us pause in the presence of God to become aware of the spiritual meaning of all that we do.

Prayers of the Faithful
We think today of people whose work is tedious or thankless. We think of those who are oppressed or exploited in their work. We think of those who want to work, but can't.

May this feast teach us that the ordinary is sacred. May we learn that our ordinary daily tasks are full of grace. May we do what we do with hopeful hearts and await God's blessing.

PHILIP AND JAMES, APOSTLES

(3 May)

Introduction to Mass
Philip and James were two of Jesus' original companions. The feast reminds us that we are Jesus' special companions today, called and entrusted with the same mission. We pause with this thought.

Prayers of the Faithful
In answer to Philip, Jesus says, 'Whoever has seen me has seen the Father'. We too encounter Jesus. May we, like Philip, come to see, ever more deeply, the fulness of God in Jesus.

James was in charge of the Church in Jerusalem, one of the very first Christian leaders. We pray for our Pope and all Christian leaders today. Lord, open their hearts, as you opened James' heart, to the Spirit.

MATTHIAS, APOSTLE

(14 May)

Introduction to Mass
Matthias was chosen to replace Judas in the twelve apostles. The reading describes him as 'one of those who accompanied us during all the time Jesus went in and out among us'. He is chosen to witness to the Resurrection. We pause for a quiet moment.

Prayers of the Faithful
In today's feast and today's gospel, may we hear God's calling of ourselves. May we, like Matthias, feel like friends and companions of Jesus. May the way we live witness to his Resurrection.

We thank God for the gift of friendship. We thank God for the friends we have. We pray that we will be friendly people – with friendly faces, friendly thoughts and friendly actions.

THE VISITATION

(31 May)

Introduction to Mass
Today's feast invites us to appreciate how God has visited all of humanity through Mary. We pause to think quietly of how God visits us now – how God comes to us in Jesus, to stay with us, to set up home with us.

Prayers of the Faithful
Mary came to Elizabeth carrying Jesus within her. May we be like Mary. May we carry Jesus in our heart. May we reach out to others with Jesus in our hearts.

Elizabeth welcomes Mary in a spirit of joy and hospitality. May hospitality be a hallmark of our community. May people find joy in our welcome.

THE SACRED HEART

(June)

Introduction to Mass
On this feast, we celebrate divine love, the love of God has given to us in Jesus and poured into our hearts by the Holy Spirit. In the peace of our hearts, let us feel ourselves bathed in divine love.

Prayers of the Faithful
We pray for our families. May the love of Jesus fill our hearts and our relationships. May all know how lovable they are in God's eyes.

We pray that, in all the ways we relate to one another, we may communicate to one another something of God's loving heart.

COLUMBA

(9 June)

Introduction to Mass
We begin with a prayer of Columba, to lead us into a moment of quiet: 'Sometimes in a lonely cell, in the presence of my God, I stand and listen. In the silence of my heart, I can hear God's will, when I listen. For I am but a servant, who is guided by my king, when I listen.'

Prayers of the Faithful
We pray for people around Ireland wherever Columba is a special saint – dioceses like Derry and Raphoe, various parishes – and also abroad, in places like Iona.

Remembering Columba, may we be inspired, in the spirit of the gospel, to give ourselves to Christ, to follow him, to live our lives for the sake of his name.

BARNABAS, APOSTLE

(11 June)

Introduction to Mass
It is said that Barnabas came closer than anybody outside the twelve to being a fully-fledged 'apostle'. He introduced Paul to the twelve – and worked very closely with Paul – including in Antioch, where the believers were first called 'Christians'. We give thanks for Barnabas today.

Prayers of the Faithful
The apostles gave him the name 'Barnabas'; it means 'son of encouragement'. It is hard to imagine a better compliment. Lord, give us a share of his spirit. May we take time and thought to encourage one another.

The Acts of the Apostles says that Barnabas was 'full of the Holy Spirit and of faith'. May we too be full of the Spirit and full of faith. May all of us live life with a positive Christian spirit.

BIRTH OF JOHN THE BAPTIST

(24 June)

Introduction to Mass
We begin our celebration of this feast with a moment of quiet with the Lord, where we ask for ourselves a share of the spirit that he gave to John.

Prayers of the Faithful
May the birth of John the Baptist help us to appreciate the wonder of our being and the wonder of our calling.

May our own children be a joy and a delight. May they grow to be courageous people with loving hearts and prophetic voices.

PETER AND PAUL, APOSTLES

(29 June)

Introduction to Mass
Peter and Paul are the two great figures of infant Christianity. We begin by asking for ourselves a share of the spirit that the Lord gave to them.

Prayers of the Faithful
May we, like Peter and Paul, be amazed at what the Lord is doing in our lives. May we share their sense of amazement at the good news of the gospel.

May the Lord raise up people in today's Church like Peter and Paul – people with the vision and faith to guide us into the future.

THOMAS, APOSTLE

(3 July)

Introduction to Mass
When the risen Lord appears to Thomas and the others, he says 'Peace be with you'. Let that peace now descend on each of us here, as we quietly bring to the Lord whatever is going on in our lives right now.

Prayers of the Faithful
'Do not doubt but believe.' In the spirit of Thomas, we ask for a strong faith, but also for a questioning faith. May we be confident to ask questions. May our questions bring us to greater faith.

Thomas is said to have preached the good news in India. So we pray for the people of India, of all religions. We pray for the well-being of Christians there. We pray for Indian people living in our own country.

BENEDICT

(11 July)

Introduction to Mass
Benedict is the great founding figure of the monastic movement that has so enriched Christianity for 1500 years. In the contemplative, monastic spirit, we enter into a moment of silent prayer.

Prayers of the Faithful
Thinking of Benedict, we pray for the gift of a contemplative spirit, for ourselves and for our world. We pray for all who cannot stop and be still. May our world learn to spend time in the presence of God.

Today we pray for the Benedictine and Cistercian monasteries in our country. We thank God for the grace of their presence in our midst. May they go on enriching the life of the Church.

MARY MAGDALENE

(22 July)

Introduction to Mass
This Mary is not the sinner who anointed Jesus' feet, nor the sister of Martha. She is the Mary who was healed by Jesus of her demons and then became one of his close companions. We pause to think how true this is of ourselves – healed by the Lord and now his close companions.

Prayers of the Faithful
Mary Magdalene was one of the few who stayed at the foot of the cross. And she was one of the first to tell the news that Jesus was risen. May we, like her, bring the hope of the gospel to others.

As one of Jesus' inner circle of disciples, Mary testifies to Jesus' equal regard for women and men. We pray that this equal regard will become more visible in our Church today.

BRIDGET OF SWEDEN

(23 July)

Introduction to Mass
Bridget is one of three women saints whom Pope John Paul II made patrons of Europe. She was canonised for her life as a mother and then a widow. So we devote our Mass today to all mothers and all widows among us.

Prayers of the Faithful
Bridget lived her Christian faith as a mother. We pray for all among us who are mothers. May their life-giving love lead to their children flourishing as human beings.

When widowed, Bridget continued to devote herself to Christian witness and founded a religious order. We pray for all who are widowed among us. May their loss also give way to new ways of being a gift to others.

JAMES, APOSTLE

(25 July)

Introduction to Mass
James was the son of Zebedee, with his brother John, and one of the very first disciples. May that very fact help us feel how close we ourselves are to the Lord. We pause for a moment.

Prayers of the Faithful
The gospel is about the spirit of service and humility that Jesus instilled in his first disciples. May the feast of James grace each one of us with a renewed sense of service.

James is venerated in Campostella and by all its pilgrims. We pray for all who make that pilgrimage across Spain. May it be for them a journey into God, a new discovery of God in their lives.

MARTHA

(29 July)

Introduction to Mass
On Martha's feast, we begin our Mass with a heartfelt prayer. In our hearts we say to the Lord what she said to him: 'Yes Lord, I believe that you are the Messiah, the Son of God, the one coming into the world'.

Prayers of the Faithful
Martha, with her brother Lazarus and her sister Mary, were a family especially close to Jesus. So we pray for our families. May we welcome Jesus as our familiar friend. May he bring peace and joy to our homes.

Jesus comforted Martha at the death of her brother Lazarus, and strengthened her faith. We pray for our family members who have died. May Jesus bring us the same comfort and reassurance.

IGNATIUS LOYOLA

(31 July)

Introduction to Mass
Ignatius founded the Society of Jesus, the Jesuit order. Five hundred years later, we praise God for the gift he has been to Christianity. Quietly, we ask God to bless us on this day.

Prayers of the Faithful
The Jesuit motto is: 'to the greater glory of God'. Today we make it our own. May all we say and all we do be said and done for the greater glory of God. May we give God glory in everything.

Ignatius is famous for the 'Spiritual Exercises' he wrote. We thank God for the enrichment they bring to so many. May all of us attend to our spiritual life. May we all grow daily in the Lord.

ALPHONSUS LIGUORI

(1 August)

Introduction to Mass
We thank God for the gift of Alphonsus. We thank God for the human face of the Church that he sought to present. We pause for a quiet moment before the loving-kindness of God.

Prayers of the Faithful
Alphonsus taught us to see Christian morality in a human way, not as something severe and legalistic. May our Church today be kind and supportive to all in their Christian living.

We pray today for the Redemptorists and Redemptoristines in Ireland. We ask the Lord to bless them and to bless all who work with them.

THE TRANSFIGURATION

(6 August)

Introduction to Mass
Today's feast recalls the special experience of the disciples, of God's glory revealed them in Christ Jesus. As we recall, we pause to thank God for the moments of revelation in our own lives.

Prayers of the Faithful
May we grow to appreciate the glory of God in the ordinary events and encounters of daily life. May the Lord open our eyes to see more clearly the wonder of our world, and the wonder in one another.

'This is my Son, my Beloved; listen to him.' May each of us take time to listen to Jesus speaking to us. As we listen, may we discover anew that we too are God's beloved, that we too are cherished by God.

DOMINIC

(8 August)

Introduction to Mass
Today we give thanks to the Lord for Dominic and for the movement he started seven hundred years ago. We give thanks too for Dominican men and women here in Ireland and ask God's blessing for them.

Prayers of the Faithful
The Dominican spirit is a combination of action and contemplation. May we each grow strong in these two sides of our Christian faith – close to God in prayer and in putting our faith into action.

The Dominicans are the Order of Preachers, modelled on Dominic's own life. We pray for all who preach or teach the Christian gospel. May their words be eloquent and inspirational.

TERESA BENEDICTA

(9 August)

Introduction to Mass
Edith Stein was canonised by John Paul II as a patron of Europe and is known as Teresa Benedicta of the Cross. A Jew who converted to Catholicism, she was captured by the Nazis and died in Auschwitz. As we remember her, we remember all victims of the Holocaust.

Prayers of the Faithful
Edith became a Carmelite nun, so we pray for all Carmelites in our country. We pray too that the contemplative spirit will flourish. May many more in our Church know the enrichment of contemplative prayer.

Edith was both Jewish and Christian. We pray for the people of the Jewish religion. We pray for ever greater peace and mutual appreciation between Christians and Jews.

LAWRENCE

(10 August)

Introduction to Mass
Lawrence was a deacon in the Church at Rome, martyred around 250 AD. Very little is known about him, but he has been held in great esteem over the centuries. We now pause to bring before the Lord our own efforts to live our faith.

Prayers of the Faithful
In the spirit of Lawrence, we pray that the greatest treasure of the Church will be those who are poor and those who are suffering. May our greatest care and preoccupation as Christians be for them.

We remember all the deacons who serve in our Christian communities, and all who are preparing to be ordained deacon. May the Lord inspire in all of us the same spirit of service.

THE ASSUMPTION

(15 August)

Introduction to Mass
On this feast we rejoice that Mary, the first of all the disciples, is united with Christ in heaven. In our hearts we now call to mind that this feast celebrates our destiny too. Where Mary has gone, we too will follow.

Prayers of the Faithful
We give thanks for the assurance that this feast brings. As Mary is united with Jesus in heaven, may we all one day be reunited with our departed family and friends.

May God, who exalted Mary in her lowliness, be the hope of all who are bowed down and the strength of all who are humble.

BARTHOLOMEW, APOSTLE

(24 August)

Introduction to Mass
Bartholomew is only mentioned once in the gospels, in the list of the apostles Jesus called together. That tells us simply that he was one of Jesus' closest companions. The feast reminds us that we are Jesus' special companions today, called and entrusted with the same mission. We pause with this thought.

Prayers of the Faithful
'Apostle' means 'sent'. Today we give thanks for one of the original apostles who shared in Jesus' mission to proclaim the gospel. We thank God for the good news of the gospel we have received.

Bartholomew has a special place of honour in Eastern Christianity. So we pray for those Orthodox Christians today. We pray for ever closer ties of friendship and peace between Eastern and Western Christianity.

AUGUSTINE

(28 August)

Introduction to Mass
Augustine, we know, went through a long process of conversion before he found God. For a quiet moment, we pray for God's Spirit for ourselves, on our own journey out of darkness into the light.

Prayers of the Faithful
We praise God today for all that Augustine has given to the Church in the 1,500 years since he lived. We give thanks for his teaching and his theology. We ask God to bless all Augustinians.

Augustine, from his experience of conversion from sin, has helped us understand God's grace. We pray that all people, in their struggle with sin, will come to know the power of God's grace.

BIRTH OF THE VIRGIN MARY

(8 September)

Introduction to Mass
We know nothing of Mary's birth, but we do know the purpose of her life – to say 'Yes' to Christ. We pause to reflect, for this is why we ourselves were born – to say 'Yes' to Christ.

Prayers of the Faithful
Each of us, like Mary, is born to accept Jesus into our lives, and to bring Jesus into the world. May this be the pattern of our lives – to welcome Jesus, to carry Jesus, to give birth to Jesus.

We pray for all those newly-born in our community. We pray for their parents and families. May they, like Mary, bring new life, joy and hope to the world.

THE HOLY CROSS

(14 September)

Introduction to Mass
We rejoice in the words of today's gospel, 'God so loved the world that he sent his only Son'. We gaze for a moment at the cross, the symbol of God's love for us.

Prayers of the Faithful
We pray for people who are carrying a cross – a cross of worry or fear, of grief or loss, of pain or failure. But we pray also for all who carry a cross of love – who endure or forego or suffer because of their love.

We pray for our dead, whom we think of now. May Jesus, lifted up on the cross, lift them up to enjoy eternal life with him.

MATTHEW, EVANGELIST

(21 September)

Introduction to Mass
Matthew is the author of one of the four gospels. On his feast, we ponder for a moment in our hearts the difference the good news of the gospel has made to our lives.

Prayers of the Faithful
Someone said that every Christian is meant to be a 'fifth gospel'. As we are enriched by Matthew's gospel, may we each reflect the good news of the gospel in our lives. May the lives we lead bring hope to others.

We thank God for the gospel of Matthew. We thank God for the unique ways in which he unveils to us the mystery of Christ. May the words of the gospel sink deep in our hearts.

VINCENT DE PAUL

(27 September)

Introduction to Mass
Today we join with all Vincentians and Daughters of Charity in celebrating Vincent de Paul. We pause for a quiet moment; we open our hearts to be inspired by his example of practical Christianity.

Prayers of the Faithful
We think of all members of the Saint Vincent de Paul Society and all the generous time they give to people who are poor or struggling. May they inspire us all to care more deeply.

We pray for the poor among us; for all who lack what they need; for all who are struggling to cope. May we not be found wanting in our solidarity and generosity.

THE ARCHANGELS

(29 September)

Introduction to Mass
We celebrate the feast of Michael, Raphael and Gabriel. The word 'angel' means message, messenger. It means that God is always communicating with us. Let us be quiet now and become aware of God, and await God's message to us in this Mass.

Prayers of the Faithful
Gabriel is the most familiar of the three archangels, from the story of the Annunciation. May each person hear the same message that Mary heard, 'rejoice, so highly favoured; the Lord is with you'.

We think of people who feel no communication with God, who feel only God's silence and distance in their lives. May nobody despair of God's presence. May all of us wait in hope.

THÉRÈSE OF LISIEUX

(1 October)

Introduction to Mass
We think today of all Carmelites in Ireland, women and men. With them, we thank God for Therese, who radiated such beauty and grace despite illness and pain. We quietly ask God for a share of her spirit.

Prayers of the Faithful
Therese died at the age of twenty-four, yet she has been such a gift to the world. We pray for young adults. May they discover with joy the gift they can be and the difference they can make.

Therese was a contemplative nun; yet she is also patron of missionaries. May each of us grow more contemplative and more missionary. May we be people of deep prayer, and people who reach out to others with God's hope and love.

GUARDIAN ANGELS

(2 October)

Introduction to Mass
Today's feast is a celebration of how each one of us, individually, from the start of our existence, is held by God, cared for by God, protected by God. We rest a moment with that thought.

Prayers of the Faithful
May all Christians share in the spirit of this day. May we take care of one another and protect one another. May others know God's own care and protection, through the care we show them.

We think of people in our society who are left uncared for. May the society we live in become more compassionate and less numb, more supportive and protective, less negligent and uncaring.

FRANCIS OF ASSISI

(4 October)

Introduction to Mass
We join with all Franciscans and Capuchins in praising God for the gift of Francis. We begin by praying quietly to be inspired by him and to be given a share of his spirit.

Prayers of the Faithful
Lord, bless us with a share of the spirit that filled Francis. Bless us with a spirit of simplicity, of humility, of service. Bless us with love for all creation, and a care for the earth we inhabit.

The Lord said to Francis: 'Rebuild my house, for it is falling down'. We pray for the revitalisation of Church and Christianity in our society. May we be inspired as Francis was.

TERESA OF AVILA

(15 October)

Introduction to Mass
Teresa is one of the great women in the history of Christianity, a reforming spirit and a great spiritual writer. We join with all Carmelites today in thanking God for her life and asking for her inspiration.

Prayers of the Faithful
We pray for a share of Teresa's spirit, for her balance of contemplation and action. May we know God deeply in our prayer. And may we know God deeply in living our Christian lives.

Teresa sought to change both herself and her Carmelite order for the better. May we be like her, always striving to change for the better and doing what we can to change our Church for the better.

LUKE, EVANGELIST

(18 October)

Introduction to Mass
Luke is the author of one of the four gospels. For a moment, we ponder in our hearts the difference the good news of the gospel has made to our lives.

Prayers of the Faithful
'The kingdom of God is very near to you.' This is the good news, the gospel, that Luke brings to us. We pray, may all God's people come to know this. We think especially of those who are poor and those who are suffering.

We thank God for the gospel of Luke, and for the unique ways in which he unveils to us the mystery of Christ. May the words of the gospel sink deep in our hearts.

SIMON AND JUDE, APOSTLES

(28 October)

Introduction to Mass
Simon and Jude were two of Jesus' original companions. The feast reminds us that we are Jesus' special companions today, called and entrusted with the same mission. We pause with this thought.

Prayers of the Faithful
In today's feast and today's gospel, may we hear God's calling of ourselves. May we, like Simon and Jude, feel like friends and companions of Jesus. May the way we live witness to his Resurrection.

We associate St Jude with 'hopeless cases'. So let us pray for all who are despairing; for all who feel that their situation or their cause is hopeless. May the God of hope breathe new spirit into them.

ALL SAINTS

(1 November)

Introduction to Mass
Our prayers today join us, who are the living saints, with all the saints who have gone before us. We pause to contemplate the mystery of who we are – members of the Communion of Saints that spans heaven and earth.

Prayers of the Faithful
The saints who have gone before us endured all the ups and downs of life. May their memory increase our courage and give us hope.

We all have our favourite saints. We thank God for them, and for the inspiration they bring us. We pray for all the inspirational figures in our lives – saints living and dead.

ALL SOULS

(2 November)

Introduction to Mass
On this sacred day, we remember all our dead. We take a moment to let their names and faces come before us. And we visualise them with confidence, in the company of God – Father, Son and Holy Spirit.

Prayers of the Faithful
May all those who have died rest in your embrace, O Lord, as they did in life. We pray for those who died in the last year in our community. We pray for family and friends who have died.

We know that each person dies just as they are. We ask you, Lord, to work through our prayers, for the forgiveness of their faults, the purification of their souls, and the completion of their journey into the arms of your everlasting love.

ALL SAINTS OF IRELAND

(6 November)

Introduction to Mass
A few days ago we celebrated All Saints. Today we celebrate all the saints of Ireland. And again today, it is a celebration of what we all are – called to belong to the Communion of Saints, a communion uniting all in heaven and all on earth.

Prayers of the Faithful
We thank God for all the saints who have meant so much for Christianity in Ireland. We think especially of our local saints, and how much they mean to us.

We pray for our country and its future. We pray for the saints of today and tomorrow, making Christianity a life-giving, hope-filled presence in Ireland.

LATERAN BASILICA

(9 November)

Introduction to Mass
The Lateran is the cathedral church of Rome and the mother of all churches. So we make our Mass today a special prayer for the Church throughout the world – for all Christians communities who gather as we do today.

Prayers of the Faithful
May the word 'church' mean more than a building. May it mean a vibrant, welcoming community – where people are alive with God's Spirit and with the hope of the gospel.

May the Church be a life-giving presence in our community. May the good news of the gospel permeate, like living water, into all parts of society.

COLUMBANUS

(23 November)

Introduction to Mass
Columbanus is one of the greatest of all Irish missionaries. His feast reminds us of the missionary impulse that all Christians are meant to share. Let us pause to reflect on our mission; our joy as Christians is only complete when we share it.

Prayers of the Faithful
We pray today for Columban missionaries, and for all Irish missionaries in different parts of the world, religious and lay people, following the call of the gospel, hearing the cries of God's people.

Missionaries like Columbanus made such a difference to Christianity and faith in Europe. We pray that Christianity in today's Europe will find new vitality. May it bring meaning and hope to people's lives.

ANDREW, APOSTLE

(30 November)

Introduction to Mass
Andrew was one of Jesus' original companions. The feast reminds us that we are Jesus' special companions today, called and entrusted with the same mission. We pause with this thought.

Prayers of the Faithful
Andrew, we are told, brought his brother Simon to Jesus. We thank the Lord for all who bring fellow family-members to Jesus – through love, through talking, through witness of life.

May we, like Andrew, be close to Jesus. May we, like Andrew, bring other people to Jesus – through the sincerity of our faith, through the light of our hope, through the gentleness of our love.

FRANCIS XAVIER

(3 December)

Introduction to Mass
Francis Xavier was one of the first Jesuits, a missionary to faraway places, Goa and Japan. So we begin by bringing into our prayer God's people in all parts of the world, for all are God's beloved.

Prayers of the Faithful
We are all missionaries. May Francis Xavier inspire us to be bearers of the good news of the gospel wherever we are. May we bring Christ's hope and healing to each other.

We pray today for Jesuits. We thank God for their ministry in education. We thank God for their making us more aware of translating faith into action for a more just world.

IMMACULATE CONCEPTION

(8 December)

Introduction to Mass
On this feast, we celebrate how Mary was graced at the core of her being from the beginning of her being. We reflect for a moment, with thanks that we too are graced by God.

Prayers of the Faithful
Today we celebrate the words, 'Hail full of grace'. We celebrate the grace that is the heart of the universe. We rejoice that we are graced at the core of our being.

Let each of us say 'Yes' with Mary. 'Let it be done to me according to your word.' May each of us say 'yes' to the power of grace in us and be freed from the power of sin.

JOHN OF THE CROSS

(14 December)

Introduction to Mass
John is one of the great contemplative figures in our Christian tradition. So it's appropriate to begin with a moment of stillness – simply being quiet and still, aware only of God.

Prayers of the Faithful
John's best known phrase is probably 'the dark night of the soul'. We pray for all who are going through spiritual struggles. May all of us know God's light, even in our darkness.

We thank God for all the enrichment John of the Cross has brought to Christianity. May all God's people grow in the spirit of contemplation, and come to know the riches it brings.

Scripture Index

In the following, wherever the same text is used on two different days during the year, it is listed separately for each occasion. Gospel references for feast days are not included.

MATTHEW

Matthew 1:1–17 (genealogy of Jesus): 17 December
Matthew 1:18–24 (Joseph): 18 December
Matthew 4:12–17, 23–25 (Jesus begins his preaching): 7 January
Matthew 5:1–12 (beatitudes): Week ten, Monday
Matthew 5:13–16 (salt, light): Week ten, Tuesday
Matthew 5:17–19 (not to abolish but to complete): Lent, week three, Wednesday
Matthew 5:17–19 (not to abolish, but to complete): Week ten, Wednesday
Matthew 5:20–26 (be reconciled): Lent, week one, Friday
Matthew 5:20–26 (be reconciled): Week ten, Thursday
Matthew 5:27–32 (adultery, divorce): Week ten, Friday
Matthew 5:33–37 (do not swear): Week ten, Saturday
Matthew 5:38–42 (the other cheek): Week eleven, Monday
Matthew 5:43–48 (love your enemies): Lent, week one, Saturday
Matthew 5:43–48 (love your enemies): Week eleven, Tuesday
Matthew 6:1–6, 16–18 (prayer, fasting, almsgiving): Ash Wednesday
Matthew 6:7–15 (our Father): Lent, week one, Tuesday
Matthew 6:7–15 (our Father): Week eleven, Thursday
Matthew 6:19–23 (where your treasure is): Week eleven, Friday
Matthew 6:24–34 (set your hearts on God's kingdom): Week eleven, Saturday
Matthew 7:1–5 (do not judge): Week twelve, Monday
Matthew 7:6, 12–14 (treat others as you would like to be treated): Week twelve, Tuesday
Matthew 7:7–12 (ask and it will be given): Lent, week one, Thursday
Matthew 7:15–20 (by their fruits): Week twelve, Wednesday
Matthew 7:21, 24–27 (house built on rock): Advent, week one, Thursday
Matthew 7:21–29 (house built on rock): Week twelve, Thursday
Matthew 8:1–4 (Jesus heals a leper): Week twelve, Friday
Matthew 8:5–11 (the centurion): Advent, week one, Monday
Matthew 8:5–17 (the centurion): Week twelve, Saturday
Matthew 8:18–22 (follow me): Week thirteen, Monday
Matthew 8:23–27 (storm on the lake): Week thirteen, Tuesday
Matthew 8:28–34 (two demoniacs): Week thirteen, Wednesday

Matthew 9:1–8 (paralysed man): Week thirteen, Thursday
Matthew 9:9–13 (eating with sinners): Week thirteen, Friday
Matthew 9:14–15 (and then they will fast): Friday after Ash Wednesday
Matthew 9:14–17 (new wineskins): Week thirteen, Saturday
Matthew 9:18–26 (two healings): Week fourteen, Monday
Matthew 9:27–31 (two blind men): Advent, week one, Friday
Matthew 9:32–38 (Jesus proclaims the good news): Week fourteen, Tuesday
Matthew 9:35–10:1, 6–8 (Jesus calls the twelve): Advent, week one, Saturday
Matthew 10:1–7 (Jesus calls the twelve): Week fourteen, Wednesday
Matthew 10:7–15 (Jesus sends the twelve): Week fourteen, Thursday
Matthew 10:16–23 (the Spirit will be speaking in you): Week fourteen, Friday
Matthew 10:24–33 (do not be afraid): Week fourteen, Saturday
Matthew 10:34–11:1 (not peace, but a sword): Week fifteen, Monday
Matthew 11:11–15 (John the Baptist): Advent, week two, Thursday
Matthew 11:16–19 (the Son of Man comes eating and drinking): Advent, week two, Friday
Matthew 11:20–24 (they refused to repent): Week fifteen, Tuesday
Matthew 11:25–27 (revealing them to mere children): Week fifteen, Wednesday
Matthew 11:28–30 (come to me): Week fifteen, Thursday
Matthew 11:28–30 (come to me): Advent, week two, Wednesday
Matthew 12:1–8 (Jesus and the Sabbath): Week fifteen, Friday
Matthew 12:14–21 (my beloved): Week fifteen, Saturday
Matthew 12:38–42 (sign of Jonah): Week sixteen, Monday
Matthew 12:46–50 (who is my mother?): Week sixteen, Tuesday
Matthew 13:1–9 (the sower): Week sixteen, Wednesday
Matthew 13:10–17 (why do you talk in parables?): Week sixteen, Thursday
Matthew 13:18–23 (the parable of the sower explained): Week sixteen, Friday
Matthew 13:24–30 (let them both grow): Week sixteen, Saturday
Matthew 13:31–35 (the mustard seed): Week seventeen, Monday
Matthew 13:36–43 (the parable of the wheat explained): Week seventeen, Tuesday
Matthew 13:44–46 (the pearl of great price): Week seventeen, Wednesday
Matthew 13:47–53 (the dragnet): Week seventeen, Thursday
Matthew 13:54–58 (the carpenter's son, surely?): Week seventeen, Friday
Matthew 14:1–12 (John the Baptist's death): Week seventeen, Saturday
Matthew 14:13–21 (the loaves and fishes): Week eighteen, Monday
Matthew 14:22–36 (the storm on the lake): Week eighteen, Tuesday
Matthew 15:21–28 (the Canaanite woman): Week eighteen, Wednesday
Matthew 15:29–37 (I feel sorry for all these people): Advent, week one, Wednesday
Matthew 16:13–23 (who do you say I am?): Week eighteen, Thursday

Matthew 16:24–28 (renounce yourself): Week eighteen, Friday
Matthew 17:10–13 (Elijah and John the Baptist): Advent, week two, Saturday
Matthew 17:14–20 (faith as a mustard seed): Week eighteen, Saturday
Matthew 17:22–27 (the half-shekel): Week nineteen, Monday
Matthew 18:1–5, 10, 12–14 (be like little children): Week nineteen, Tuesday
Matthew 18:12–14 (the lost sheep): Advent, week two, Tuesday
Matthew 18:15–20 (if your brother does something wrong): Week nineteen, Wednesday
Matthew 18:21–35 (how often must I forgive?): Lent, week three, Tuesday
Matthew 18:21–19:1 (forgiveness): Week nineteen, Thursday
Matthew 19:3–12 (divorce): Week nineteen, Friday
Matthew 19:13–15 (Jesus welcomes children): Week nineteen, Saturday
Matthew 19:16–22 (rich young man): Week twenty, Monday
Matthew 19:23–30 (for God, everything is possible): Week twenty, Tuesday
Matthew 20:1–16 (the workers in the vineyard): Week twenty, Wednesday
Matthew 20:17–28 (the sons of Zebedee): Lent, week two, Wednesday
Matthew 21:23–27 (what authority have you?): Advent, week three, Monday
Matthew 21:28–32 (the two sons): Advent, week three, Tuesday
Matthew 21:33–43, 45–46 (the stone rejected by the builders): Lent, week two, Friday
Matthew 22:1–14 (the wedding feast): Week twenty, Thursday
Matthew 22:34–40 (love God, love your neighbour): Week twenty, Friday
Matthew 23:1–12 (you have only one Teacher): Lent, week two, Tuesday
Matthew 23:1–12 (you have only one Teacher): Week twenty, Saturday
Matthew 23:13–22 (blind guides): Week twenty-one, Monday
Matthew 23:23–26 (clean the inside): Week twenty-one, Tuesday
Matthew 23:27–32 (hypocrisy): Week twenty-one, Wednesday
Matthew 24:42–51 (be ready): Week twenty-one, Thursday
Matthew 25:1–13 (ten bridesmaids): Week twenty-one, Friday
Matthew 25:14–30 (the talents): Week twenty-one, Saturday
Matthew 25:31–46 (the sheep and the goats): Lent, week one, Monday
Matthew 26:14–25 (Judas): Holy Week, Wednesday
Matthew 28:8–15 (awe and great joy): Easter Monday

MARK

Mark 1:14–20 (believe the good news; follow me): Week one, Monday
Mark 1:21–28 (he teaches with authority; unclean spirit): Week one, Tuesday

Mark 1:29–39 (Jesus heals many; he goes off to pray): Week one, Wednesday
Mark 1:40–45 (a leper): Week one, Thursday
Mark 2:1–12 (the paralytic): Week one, Friday
Mark 2:13–17 (Jesus' table fellowship): Week one, Saturday
Mark 2:18–22 (new wineskins): Week two, Monday
Mark 2:23–28 (master of the Sabbath): Week two, Tuesday
Mark 3:1–6 (man with withered hand): Week two, Wednesday
Mark 3:7–12 (crowding forward to touch him): Week two, Thursday
Mark 3:13–19 (calling the twelve): Week two, Friday
Mark 3:20–21 (out of his mind): Week two, Saturday
Mark 3:22–30 (Beelzebul, sin against Spirit): Week three, Monday
Mark 3:31–35 (my brother and sister and mother): Week three, Tuesday
Mark 4:1–20 (the sower): Week three, Wednesday
Mark 4:21–25 (the lamp, the measure): Week three, Thursday
Mark 4:26–34 (parables of seeds): Week three, Friday
Mark 4:35–41 (calming the storm): Week three, Saturday
Mark 5:1–20 (unclean spirits): Week four, Monday
Mark 5:21–43 (Jairus' daughter): Week four, Tuesday
Mark 6:1–6 (amazed at their lack of faith): Week four, Wednesday
Mark 6:7–13 (the twelve sent out in pairs): Week four, Thursday
Mark 6:14–29 (beheading of John the Baptist): Week four, Friday
Mark 6:30–34 (rest for a while): Week four, Saturday
Mark 6:34–44 (loaves and fishes): 8 January
Mark 6:45–52 (walking on water): 9 January
Mark 6:53–56 (all who touched him were cured): Week five, Monday
Mark 7:1–13 (God's word and human traditions): Week five, Tuesday
Mark 7:14–23 (what comes from the heart): Week five, Wednesday
Mark 7:24–30 (Syro–Phoenician woman): Week five, Thursday
Mark 7:31–37 (*ephphatha;* be opened): Week five, Friday
Mark 8:1–10 (feeding of the four thousand): Week five, Saturday
Mark 8:11–13 (no sign shall be given): Week six, Monday
Mark 8:14–21 (do you not yet understand?): Week six, Tuesday
Mark 8:22–26 (blind man): Week six, Wednesday
Mark 8:27–33 (you are the Christ): Week six, Thursday
Mark 8:34–9:1 (take up your cross): Week six, Friday
Mark 9:2–13 (transfiguration): Week six, Saturday
Mark 9:14–29 (help my unbelief): Week seven, Monday
Mark 9:30–37 (last of all and servant of all): Week seven, Tuesday
Mark 9:38–40 (anyone not against us is for us): Week seven, Wednesday
Mark 9:41–50 (if your hand should cause you to sin): Week seven, Thursday
Mark 10:1–12 (divorce): Week seven, Friday

SCRIPTURE INDEX

Mark 10:13–16 (let the little children come to me): Week seven, Saturday
Mark 10:17–27 (the rich man): Week eight, Monday
Mark 10:28–31 (what about us?): Week eight, Tuesday
Mark 10:32–45 (the Son of Man came to serve): Week eight, Wednesday
Mark 10:46–52 (Bartimaeus): Week eight, Thursday
Mark 11:11–26 (Jesus clears the temple): Week eight, Friday
Mark 11:27–33 (Jesus' authority): Week eight, Saturday
Mark 12:1–12 (he sent his beloved son): Week nine, Monday
Mark 12:13–17 (give to Caesar what belongs to Caesar): Week nine, Tuesday
Mark 12:18–27 (God is God of the living): Week nine, Wednesday
Mark 12:28–34 (love God, love your neighbour): Week nine, Thursday
Mark 12:28–34 (love God: love your neighbour): Lent, week three, Friday
Mark 12:35–37 (Christ is the Son of David): Week nine, Friday
Mark 12:38–44 (the poor widow): Week nine, Saturday
Mark 16:9–15 (go out to the whole world): Easter Saturday

LUKE

Luke 1:5–25 (Zechariah and Elizabeth): 19 December
Luke 1:26–38 (angel Gabriel visits Mary): 20 December
Luke 1:39–45 (visitation): 21 December
Luke 1:46–56 (magnificat): 22 December
Luke 1:57–66 (birth of John the Baptist): 23 December
Luke 1:67–79 (benedictus): 24 December
Luke 2:22–35 (Simeon): 29 December
Luke 2:36–40 (Anna): 30 December
Luke 4:14–22 (the Spirit of the Lord has been given to me): 10 January
Luke 4:16–30 (good news): Week twenty-two, Monday
Luke 4:24–30 (no prophet is accepted in their own country): Lent, week three, Monday
Luke 4:31–37 (astonishment seized them): Week twenty-two, Tuesday
Luke 4:38–44 (suffering): Week twenty-two, Wednesday
Luke 5:1–11 (call of the first disciples): Week twenty-two, Thursday
Luke 5:12–16 (a leper): 11 January
Luke 5:17–26 (paralysed man): Advent, week two, Monday
Luke 5:27–32 (eating with tax-collectors and sinners): Saturday after Ash Wednesday
Luke 5:33–39 (new wine, fresh skins): Week twenty-two, Friday

Luke 6:1–5 (master of the Sabbath): Week twenty-two, Saturday
Luke 6:6–11 (stretch out your hand): Week twenty-three, Monday
Luke 6:12–19 (the twelve apostles): Week twenty-three, Tuesday
Luke 6:20–26 (how happy are you): Week twenty-three, Wednesday
Luke 6:27–38 (be compassionate): Week twenty-three, Thursday
Luke 6:36–38 (be compassionate): Lent, week two, Monday
Luke 6:39–42 (seeing clearly): Week twenty-three, Friday
Luke 6:43–49 (true foundations): Week twenty-three, Saturday
Luke 7:1–10 (the centurion): Week twenty-four, Monday
Luke 7:11–17 (widow of Nain): Week twenty-four, Tuesday
Luke 7:19–23 (tell John what you have seen): Advent, week three, Wednesday
Luke 7:24–30 (no one greater than John): Advent, week three, Thursday
Luke 7:31–35 (the Son of Man comes eating and drinking): Week twenty-four, Wednesday
Luke 7:36–50 (she covered his feet with kisses): Week twenty-four, Thursday
Luke 8:1–3 (as well as certain women): Week twenty-four, Friday
Luke 8:4–15 (the parable of the sower): Week twenty-four, Saturday
Luke 8:16–18 (so that people may see the light): Week twenty-five, Monday
Luke 8:19–21 (my mother and brothers): Week twenty-five, Tuesday
Luke 9:1–6 (Jesus sends out the twelve): Week twenty-five, Wednesday
Luke 9:7–9 (Herod asks about Jesus): Week twenty-five, Thursday
Luke 9:18–22 (who do you say I am?): Week twenty-five, Friday
Luke 9:22–25 (if anyone wants to be a follower of mine): Thursday after Ash Wednesday
Luke 9:43–45 (they did not understand him): Week twenty-five, Saturday
Luke 9:46–50 (the least is the one who is great): Week twenty-six, Monday
Luke 9:51–56 (Jesus resolutely took the road): Week twenty-six, Tuesday
Luke 9:57–62 (follow me): Week twenty-six, Wednesday
Luke 10:1–12 (Jesus sends out seventy-two others): Week twenty-six, Thursday
Luke 10:13–16 (repentance): Week twenty-six, Friday
Luke 10:17–24 (happy the eyes): Week twenty-six, Saturday
Luke 10:21–24 (happy the eyes): Advent, week one, Tuesday
Luke 10:25–37 (the good Samaritan): Week twenty-seven, Monday
Luke 10:38–42 (Martha and Mary): Week twenty-seven, Tuesday
Luke 11:1–4 (our Father): Week twenty-seven, Wednesday
Luke 11:5–13 (persistent prayer): Week twenty-seven, Thursday
Luke 11:14–23 (the finger of God): Lent, week three, Thursday
Luke 11:15–26 (the finger of God): Week twenty-seven, Friday
Luke 11:27–28 (still happier those): Week twenty-seven, Saturday
Luke 11:29–32 (the sign of Jonah): Lent, week one, Wednesday
Luke 11:29–32 (the sign of Jonah): Week twenty-eight, Monday

Luke 11:37–41 (give alms from what you have): Week twenty-eight, Tuesday
Luke 11:42–46 (alas for you Pharisees): Week twenty-eight, Wednesday
Luke 11:47–54 (alas for you lawyers): Week twenty-eight, Thursday
Luke 12:1–7 (every hair on your head): Week twenty-eight, Friday
Luke 12:8–12 (the Spirit will teach you): Week twenty-eight, Saturday
Luke 12:13–21 (rich in the sight of God): Week twenty-nine, Monday
Luke 12:35–38 (be ready): Week twenty-nine, Tuesday
Luke 12:39–48 (the faithful servant): Week twenty-nine, Wednesday
Luke 12:49–53 (I have come to bring fire): Week twenty-nine, Thursday
Luke 12:54–59 (how to interpret these times): Week twenty-nine, Friday
Luke 13:1–9 (unless you repent): Week twenty-nine, Saturday
Luke 13:10–17 (bound these eighteen years): Week thirty, Monday
Luke 13:18–21 (what is the kingdom of God like?): Week thirty, Tuesday
Luke 13:22–30 (from east and west, north and south): Week thirty, Wednesday
Luke 13:31–35 (I must go on): Week thirty, Thursday
Luke 14:1–6 (healing on the Sabbath): Week thirty, Friday
Luke 14:1, 7–11 (places of honour): Week thirty, Saturday
Luke 14:12–14 (invite the poor): Week thirty-one, Monday
Luke 14:15–24 (a great banquet): Week thirty-one, Tuesday
Luke 14:25–33 (work out the cost): Week thirty-one, Wednesday
Luke 15:1–10 (lost sheep, lost coin): Week thirty-one, Thursday
Luke 15:1–3, 11–32 (the prodigal son): Lent, week two, Saturday
Luke 16:1–8 (the astute steward): Week thirty-one, Friday
Luke 16:9–15 (use of money): Week thirty-one, Saturday
Luke 16:19–31 (the rich man and Lazarus): Lent, week two, Thursday
Luke 17:1–6 (increase our faith): Week thirty-two, Monday
Luke 17:7–10 (we are merely servants): Week thirty-two, Tuesday
Luke 17:11–19 (ten lepers): Week thirty-two, Wednesday
Luke 17:20–25 (the kingdom of God is among you): Week thirty-two, Thursday
Luke 17:26–37 (when the day comes): Week thirty-two, Friday
Luke 18:1–8 (never lost heart): Week thirty-two, Saturday
Luke 18:9–14 (the Pharisee and the publican): Lent, week three, Saturday
Luke 18:35–43 (a blind man): Week thirty-three, Monday
Luke 19:1–10 (Zacchaeus): Week thirty-three, Tuesday
Luke 19:11–28 (the ten pounds): Week thirty-three, Wednesday
Luke 19:41–44 (Jesus weeps over Jerusalem): Week thirty-three, Thursday
Luke 19:45–48 (Jesus clears the temple): Week thirty-three, Friday
Luke 20:27–40 (God of the living): Week thirty-three, Saturday
Luke 21:1–4 (the poor widow): Week thirty-four, Monday
Luke 21:5–11 (the end is not so soon): Week thirty-four, Tuesday
Luke 21:12–19 (endurance): Week thirty-four, Wednesday

Luke 21:20–28 (your liberation is near at hand): Week thirty-four, Thursday
Luke 21:29–33 (my words will never pass away): Week thirty-four, Friday
Luke 21:34–36 (stay awake): Week thirty-four, Saturday
Luke 24:13–35 (Emmaus): Easter Wednesday
Luke 24:35–48 (peace be with you): Easter Thursday

JOHN

John 1:1–18 (the Word): 31 December
John 1:19–28 (John the Baptist): 2 January
John 1:29–34 (lamb of God): 3 January
John 1:35–42 (come and see): 4 January
John 1:43–51 (Philip, Nathanael): 5 January
John 3:1–8 (you must be born from above): Easter, week two, Monday
John 3:7–15 (the wind blows where it pleases): Easter, week two, Tuesday
John 3:16–21 (God loves the world so much): Easter, week two, Wednesday
John 3:22–30 (he must grow greater): 12 January
John 3:31–36 (the Father loves the Son): Easter, week two, Thursday
John 4:43–54 (the court official's son): Lent, week four, Monday
John 5:1–3, 5–16 (the man by the pool): Lent, week four, Tuesday
John 5:17–30 (whoever believes has eternal life): Lent, week four, Wednesday
John 5:31–47 (you refuse to accept me): Lent, week four, Thursday
John 5:33–36 (John was a lamp): Advent, week three, Friday
John 6:1–15 (the loaves and fishes): Easter, week two, Friday
John 6:16–21 (Jesus walking on the lake): Easter, week two, Saturday
John 6:22–29 (look for food that endures): Easter, week three, Monday
John 6:30–35 (I am the bread of life): Easter, week three, Tuesday
John 6:35–40 (I am the bread of life): Easter, week three, Wednesday
John 6:44–51 (I am the living bread): Easter, week three, Thursday
John 6:52–59 (my flesh is real food): Easter, week three, Friday
John 6:60–69 (who shall we go to?): Easter, week three, Saturday
John 7:1–2, 10, 25–30 (there is one who sent me): Lent, week four, Friday
John 7:40–52 (there has never been anybody who spoke like this): Lent, week four, Saturday
John 8:1–11 (the woman in adultery): Lent, week five, Monday
John 8:12–20 (I am the light of the world): Lent, week five, Monday
John 8:21–30 (I am from above): Lent, week five, Tuesday
John 8:31–42 (the truth will make you free): Lent, week five, Wednesday

John 8:51–59 (before Abraham was, I am): Lent, week five, Thursday
John 10:1–10 (I have come that they may have life): Easter, week four, Monday
John 10:11–18 (the good shepherd): Easter, week four, Monday
John 10:22–30 (the Father and I are one): Easter, week four, Tuesday
John 10:31–42 (the Father is in me as I am in the Father): Lent, week five, Friday
John 11:45–57 (it is better for one man to die): Lent, week five, Saturday
John 12:1–11 (Mary anoints Jesus' feet): Holy Week, Monday
John 12:44–50 (I, the light): Easter, week four, Wednesday
John 13:1–15 (Jesus washes his disciples' feet): Holy Thursday
John 13:21–33, 36–38 (one of you will betray me): Holy Week, Tuesday
John 14:1–6 (I am the way, the truth and the life): Easter, week four, Friday
John 14:7–14 (to have seen me is to have seen the Father): Easter, week four, Saturday
John 14:21–26 (Jesus makes his home with us): Easter, week five, Monday
John 14:27–31 (peace I give you): Easter, week five, Tuesday
John 15:1–8 (I am the vine): Easter, week five, Wednesday
John 15:9–11 (remain in my love): Easter, week five, Thursday
John 15:12–17 (love one another): Easter, week five, Friday
John 15:18–21 (you do not belong to the world): Easter, week five, Saturday
John 15:26–16:4 (the Spirit of truth): Easter, week six, Monday
John 16:5–11 (I will send the Advocate): Easter, week six, Tuesday
John 16:12–15 (the Spirit of truth will lead you): Easter, week six, Wednesday
John 16:16–20 (your sorrow will turn to joy): Easter, week six, Thursday
John 16:20–23 (your hearts will be full of joy): Easter, week six, Friday
John 16:23–28 (the Father loves you for loving me): Easter, week six, Saturday
John 16:29–33 (be brave): Easter, week seven, Monday
John 17:1–11 (I pray for them): Easter, week seven, Tuesday
John 17:11–19 (consecrate them in the truth): Easter, week seven, Wednesday
John 17:20–26 (may they all be one): Easter, week seven, Thursday
John 20:11–18 (Mary of Magdala sees the Lord): Easter Tuesday
John 21:1–14 (Jesus appears by the lake): Easter Friday
John 21:15–19 (do you love me?): Easter, week seven, Friday
John 21:20–25 (you are to follow me): Easter, week seven, Saturday